# Negotiating
# Secrets
## The experts tell all!

About the author
David Brown MCIPD studied
mechanical engineering at
Loughborough University
and secured a diploma in
Management Studies from the
University of Aston. He has
over 30 years' experience of
negotiating business contracts,
and for the last 20 years has
been a consultant and coach
specializing in improving
business performance. He has
a diploma in Neuro Linguistic
Programming (NLP), which
offers insight into behaviours
associated with negotiating.
For more information visit
www.scott-brown.co.uk

# Negotiating
# secrets

**Collins**
A division of HarperCollins*Publishers*
77-85 Fulham Palace Road, London W6 8JB

www.BusinessSecrets.net

First published in Great Britain in 2010 by HarperCollins*Publishers*
Published in Canada by HarperCollins*Canada*. www.harpercollins.ca
Published in Australia by HarperCollins*Australia*. www.harpercollins.com.au
Published in India by HarperCollins*PublishersIndia*. www.harpercollins.co.in

1

A catalogue record for this book is available from the British Library.

ISBN 978-0-00-732807-9

Printed and bound at Clays Ltd, St Ives plc

# Contents

# Skilful negotiating will improve your life

Many people think that negotiating is just about money and business. It isn't. We do it instinctively, as children, in our families, and in our communities as well as in business, management, industrial relations and all levels of government. Sometimes we negotiate without realizing it.

I first woke up to negotiating as a young sales manager 35 years ago. Since then I have modified the framework, and learnt as I have gone along. I have collected best practice from all over the world, run training courses on the subject, negotiated with trade unions, and worked with my clients as they have reached agreements with both their employees and customers. I have seen people make all the classic mistakes because they don't know how to negotiate effectively. I've also seen the other side – the huge benefits that come from good negotiating.

This book captures all that experience in the form of 50 **secrets** presented over seven chapters. If you use these **secrets** they will help you seize opportunities, make more money, develop relationships and maximize what you will achieve with the rest of your life. The chapters are:

■ **Know when to negotiate.** There are alternatives to negotiation. Before you start, you need to be sure what is meant by negotiation, and what the alternatives are.

■ **Prepare clear objectives.** If you know what you want to finish up with, then you are halfway there.

■ **Discuss your respective positions.** Reaching agreement is much more likely if each party understands where the other is coming from. This is about setting the scene – listening more than you talk, before you propose anything.

■ **Deal only in packages.** You can't bargain if you only talk about one thing. You just argue. This chapter shows you how to reach agreement by trading packages.

■ **Bargain your way to success.** Once you have exchanged packages, then you bargain (compromise) your way to agreement. There may be several stages to this.

■ **Find common ground.** You don't want to move apart. You do want to reach agreement and come together. Here's how.

■ **Put it all together.** This is a summary of the key secrets and the ideas behind them. They are all important, but this chapter will help you decide on the most important factors in the specific situations that you will find yourself.

Whether you are engaged in buying, selling, industrial relations, domestic disputes or family matters, you are negotiating more often than you realize. Sometimes you will negotiate with someone just once and never see them again. More often we negotiate with people who we have an ongoing relationship with, and we want them to come back to the negotiating table with good feelings towards us.

## Follow these secrets so that you can negotiate sucessfully in any situation.

# Know when to negotiate

**Negotiating** is about 'give and take'. It is a means by which we compromise and agree a way forward. This chapter looks at how you can decide whether to negotiate or use some other process. It also emphasizes the importance of achieving outcomes satisfactory to both parties. In most negotiations we want the other party to feel comfortable with what has been agreed so we can move forward and develop an ongoing relationship that is valuable to both of us.

# 1.1

# Be clear what negotiating is

If you are to be good at negotiating, you need to know what it is, and what it is not. It is not selling; it is a system of 'give and take' that allows two parties to reach agreement. It is about compromise.

Many people confuse selling with negotiating, and this is likely to make them poor sellers and poor negotiators. If you sell, you are persuading a customer that they want something. You negotiate with them then you agree how much it is worth, how many they will have, when you will deliver it, and the payment terms that will apply. In other words you will agree, or negotiate, a package.

The concept of packages is crucial to understanding negotiation. If the only thing you discuss is price, you can't negotiate. You will simply

**one minute wonder** Look at today's newspaper. It will contain many stories that involve negotiating. World leaders will be negotiating with one another; companies will be negotiating with their employees, and opposing sides in wars – with luck – will be negotiating peace.

> **"Man is an animal that makes bargains; no other animal does this – no dog exchanges bones with another"**
> **Adam Smith, Scottish economist, author of The Wealth of Nations**

haggle or argue. When you introduce two or more variables, you have a package on which you can reach a mutually acceptable compromise.

To fully understand what negotiating means you have to appreciate that in most business situations you don't negotiate with someone just once in your life. Usually, you will negotiate with them many times, possibly over many years. So it is helpful to think of those that we negotiate with as a partner.

Usually you need your negotiating partners to leave a negotiation with you feeling that they've 'won'. Of course, you want to win too. When both parties feel that they have won, this is called win-win.

So, to help you understand what negotiation is, I have introduced a few key ideas that will be fully developed later in this book:

- **Give and take.** This is the essence of negotiating.
- **Packages.** These are what you deal in.
- **Partner.** This is who you negotiate with.
- **Win-win.** This is how you want to end up, with both parties happy and ready to do business with each other again.

Hopefully, you will recognize that these ideas are not just the stuff of reaching commercial agreement – they also allow communities to thrive and allow us to co-exist as human beings.

This book will show that you negotiate more often than you realize. Once you realize you are doing it, you will be more successful.

## Before you start negotiating, be clear that you are prepared to 'give and take'.

# 1.2

# Consider alternatives to negotiating

You are trying to reach a commercial agreement, secure an industrial relations agreement, solve a problem or resolve a dispute. Negotiation should take place when you need somebody's consent to a proposal, and they need yours before you decide to agree. But you should only negotiate if negotiation is the best way to achieve your objectives.

Consider that there are many alternatives to negotiating, and in some situations they may give you a better result.

■ **Persuade.** Persuade them that what you are proposing is the best option. This is a buying or selling approach that might be used in connection with a price rise or one of the terms of the contract. It doesn't cost you money.

■ **Impose.** Just tell them what they must do, or what you must do (you could say you have no choice). Shops are effectively doing this when they offer goods on a non-negotiable basis. Sometimes price rises or purchasing conditions are presented as non-negotiable.

■ **Instruct.** It's a less severe form of impose, but you are still dictating the terms if you choose to do this.

■ **Postpone.** Put it off till circumstances change. An example of this would be putting off price rises or reductions in a commodity such as oil or metals, because the short-term situation is too volatile. You could choose to allow the market to settle down.

■ **Leave it to chance.** Allow the situation to be dictated by outside events, such as linking a price to the dollar or inflation.

■ **Give in.** This is an option, but not one you will enjoy. Sometimes governments, companies or individuals have to give in because the odds are 100% against them.

■ **Problem solve.** If both parties can work on solving the same problem this may be a good idea. Employers and a trade union might co-operate to decide how best to deal with a financial crisis.

■ **Arbitrate.** Allow another person or body to solve this for you. An industrial tribunal could resolve an industrial dispute.

■ **Plead.** Rely on an appeal to someone's good nature. This is only a good idea if you can rely on their good nature, or if it's not important to you.

Whether one of these alternatives is a better option than negotiating depends on many factors – you, your boss, your negotiating partner's circumstances, the market in which you operate, the short term, the long term, your confidence levels and risk, to name but a few. We will study these options in more detail in 1.3 and give you ideas on how to decide on the best option.

# Before you embark on any negotiation, be sure to recognize that there may be better ways of solving the problem.

# 1.3

# Decide if negotiating is your best bet

There is no point in using brilliant negotiating skills if you shouldn't be negotiating. In 1.2 we listed the main alternatives to negotiating. Here we will explore the advantages and disadvantages of those approaches.

■ **Persuade.** If you can persuade them to your point of view, you've no need to negotiate. On the other hand, it can take forever. It won't succeed if there is a serious clash of interests – if for instance your partner's position in the market place is badly affected.

■ **Impose.** This can save you time and money, but it may ruin long-term relationships. Your partner may decide that you have stopped thinking win-win and are thinking only of yourself.

---

**case study** As a sales manager, I regularly negotiated a large contract to supply aluminium products to a US-owned company. One year we agreed to use an American source of primary ingot as the basis of our costs. We neglected to consider the possibility that our costs might shoot through the roof because of changes in the dollar-sterling exchange rate. We took

---

■ **Instruct.** It's quick, but people like to be offered choices, so are put off by being told what's going to happen.

■ **Postpone.** A good idea if the problem might go away, or if you think conditions will change in your favour. A bad idea if conditions change for the worse.

■ **Leave it to chance.** A good idea if it seems fair. A bad idea if one party suffers so much that the agreement is sunk.

■ **Give in.** A good idea if you have no choice whatsoever – it's going to happen anyway. A bad idea if it destroys your credibility or if it will cost you in the long term.

■ **Problem solve.** A good idea if you can work together on the same problem. A bad idea if each party has a seriously different agenda.

■ **Arbitrate.** A good idea if both parties will accept the outcome. A bad idea if one party will be unhappy with the decision of the arbitrator.

■ **Plead.** It shows you in a conciliatory light, as someone who is reasonable. But it puts you at the mercy of others, and may make you appear weak.

Once you have considered these options, but have then decided that negotiating is your best bet, we can focus on the techniques that will allow you to negotiate successfully.

# Consider the advantages and disadvantages of alternatives to negotiating before embarking on a negotiation.

a chance on there not being a significant change in the exchange rate. Months later there was a massive change, and our hard-won agreement was put at risk – we had left one major issue to chance. After that, we learnt to put exchange rate limits in all our agreements, and negotiated a mechanism that kicked in outside those limits.

# 1.4

# Know who you are dealing with

Whether we seek to impose a decision on someone, or leave things flexible, or negotiate, depends on the other party as much as on us. If you are to succeed, whatever you decide to do must depend to a large extent on who you are dealing with.

These are some of the things that you need to consider about the other party when negotiating:

■ **Expectations.** What are their expectations going to be? Why do they have those expectations?

■ **Behaviour.** How will they expect you to behave? How will they behave? Are they naturally aggressive, or conciliatory? Will they make

**case study** I used to negotiate regularly with an Indian family that had a significant position within the aluminium industry in Europe. Whichever member of the family I negotiated with, I needed to recognize that they would always inflate the volumes that they were going to take in order to get the best price. They talked big and took a lot smaller. I had to develop a strategy

extreme demands or will they be more reasonable? Will they react in a logical way or will they expect you to behave in a particular way, because that's the way you have behaved in the past? If you suddenly behave differently, how will they react – will it increase or reduce your chances of reaching agreement?

■ **Culture.** What culture do they come from? We will return to this in 1.6, and elsewhere – because understanding their background is a vital part of understanding what will appeal to them and what will turn them off. This will be the difference between success and failure.

■ **Preferences.** Will they want to negotiate one-on-one or will they turn up as a team? Is the other party likely to see the world through positive or negative eyes? Is their glass half full or half empty? Do they look at the big picture or the detail?

■ **Pressures.** Even if they turn up on their own, has their boss exerted pressure on them to get a particular result? If there are such pressures on the other party, I would call this 'having a monkey on their back' and you need to be aware of it.

■ **Options.** How important are you to them? How important is it for them to reach agreement? What's their best alternative to reaching agreement?

# Understand who you are dealing with and be sensitive about them and their situation.

that coped with this. One tactic I used was to go right back to square one with a fresh package for the reduced volume. That was not well received. Instead I made sure that my concessions on specification and price were still going to be acceptable to me when the volumes inevitably started to reduce, and I built that into my first package.

# 1.5

# Aim for win-win outcomes

Whether you are a buyer, a seller, or involved in industrial relations, you will usually negotiate with the same people on a regular basis. You will want to develop a relationship with them so that they want to do business with you again. You will both want to feel that you have made a good agreement – we call this feeling 'win-win'.

We are going to consider outcomes – the end results of negotations. It is crucially important to know your own objectives – where you want to finish up – before you set off. There are four possible outcomes to any negotiation:

**1** **Failure to agree.** When it is appropriate for the negotiators to go their separate ways, because there is simply nothing on which they can possibly agree.

## "Begin with the end in mind"
**Stephen Covey, author of The Seven Habits of Highly Effective People**

**2** **Lose-lose.** When both parties refuse to move, when it was in both their interests to do so. Neither side achieves its objectives nor do the two parties generate solutions to their problems. This leads to total disillusion and frustration with the negotiation process and a danger of souring long-term relationships through a loss of respect and trust. When they come to reflect on this after the event, both parties are likely to regard it as an opportunity missed and will not be proud of themselves.

**3** **Win-lose.** When movement is predominately one-sided. The side that did not move 'wins' whilst the side that did all the moving 'loses'. In a win-lose situation, individuals are usually more concerned with victory rather than relationships. Too much effort is put into achieving short-term goals rather than long-term objectives. A 'them and us' attitude is created and the long-term relationship between the parties is jeopardized.

**4** **Win-win.** The experienced negotiator will work towards creating two-way movement that is felt to be reasonably split between the two sides. Movement is aimed at bridging any gaps between them. During the negotiation, channels are developed and kept open for two-way communication. With an emphasis on flexibility, solutions are proposed that enable both sides to achieve their objectives. Satisfactory decisions are arrived at and long-term relationships are enhanced. There is a perception that both parties have demonstrated reasonable movement, the lifeblood of negotiations. Once the meeting is finished, there is a spirit of partnership as the two parties set about making the agreement work.

# If you want to do business with someone in future, aim for a win-win result from every negotiation.

# 1.6

# Learn to deal with different cultures

I would define culture as 'the way we do things around here'. What is meant by 'around here'? It means wherever in the world you are doing business. To succeed as a negotiator you need to understand where the other party is coming from.

It is very dangerous to generalize on the subject of culture – you could say there are as many cultures as people you deal with. The important thing is to be prepared for others to think and behave differently from you. The usual advice for dealing with the Japanese is to be very, very patient. Yet no culture is entirely predictable, so don't be surprised when you encounter some Japanese who expect you to hurry up!

**case study** The Japanese have a very special approach to negotiating. In my experience they are very difficult to read (like good poker players) and frequently need the approval of their colleagues on key issues. I have negotiated with Japanese agents over substantial supplies of aluminium sheet for making freight containers. As negotiators, they are not aggres-

> **"If you negotiate with Japanese clients, ask questions. When you think you understand, ask more questions"**
>
> **John L Graham, professor of business, University of California**

Nor can you make generalizations about gender differences. When men are negotiating with women, some feel a gentle approach is called for, but many women will object to being patronized in this way. Some women want to prove themselves better than men, and will therefore prove as combative as any man.

Some businesses have reputations for being aggressive in everything they do – in employing people, in buying, and in selling. If you deal with them, your tactics need to be adjusted to suit theirs – with an aggressive first offer for instance. Other companies that you will deal with have an approach that is very much concerned with respecting the rights of their employees or their suppliers. You simply have to know who you are dealing with!

## Your negotiating partner's behaviour may be very different to your own, so be prepared to allow for this.

sive, but patient and firm. The specific Japanese approach that I would like to share with you is their tendency to go over the same ground again and again. Once at 6:00pm, I felt we were minutes from agreement. We had been hard at it for three hours. I should have known when they said "can we just check on the specification" that it would take another four hours!

# Prepare clear objectives

**The old maxim** 'proper preparation prevents poor performance' is as crucial in negotiating as it is in presentations, sales visits and other areas of business. This chapter provides you with a preparation framework that allows you to define your objectives, anticipate the other party's approach, and develop your own strategy and tactics. Thus prepared, you have a much better chance of reaching an agreement satisfactory to both sides.

# 2.1

# Plan your approach

A clear understanding of your objectives is essential when negotiating. You should be ready to propose a package that is challenging but credible. Your preparation should end with you deciding on your 'Desirable' list and using it to form the basis of your first proposal. Use these steps to prepare.

**1** List the things on which you can give and take. These are called your negotiating variables. If it is possible to give and take on something, list it as a variable.

**2** For each variable, list the 'Desirable' (best you can hope for), 'Probable' (most likely) and 'Worst' (worst that you would want to finish up with) outcome from your point of view.

**3** Put a value on the difference between 'Desirable' and 'Worst'. Now you have identified what the most valuable items are from your point of view. Price and volume are obvious values, but sometimes it is more difficult to put a value on a variable.

**4** List all those things on which you are not prepared to give and take. You are effectively saying they are non-negotiable.

**5** Look at everything done so far from the point of view of the other party. Ask yourself what they will be looking for on each variable – and what variables they will be looking at.

**6** Consider where you will have areas of agreement, and where there will be disagreement. If your partner wants to negotiate on the things that you have considered to be non-negotiable, you may struggle to reach agreement.

**7** Having weighed up the situation, you should be prepared to propose your first package (see chapter 4) as the 'Desirable' set of objectives, although the Discussion (chapter 3) may cause you to modify your first proposal.

### Example list of negotiating variables

This table shows how selling a family business looked when listed in the way described. Your preparation will always give you maximum support if you finish up with this sort of five-column table.

| Negotiating variable | Desirable | Probable | Worst | Likely difference in value desirable to worst |
|---|---|---|---|---|
| Basic price (for 100%) | £5.1m | £4.7m | £4.5m | £600,000 |
| Keep a family stake | 30% | 20% | 10% | £1m |
| Retain directors | Father = MD Son = Prod Dir | Father retires Son = Prod Dir | Both retire | Pride and/or renumeration |
| Pay directors | 2 years at £30k each | 1 year at £30k | Nil | £120,000 |
| Retain staff | Maintain status quo for 6 months | 3 months' notice clause | 3 months' notice clause | Loyalty |
| Payment terms | 100% now | 50% now 50% two months | 100% two months | Security and interest |

# Prepare a detailed list of variables and assess their importance to both parties.

# 2.2

# Anticipate the other party's approach

In your preparation, it is important to consider the likely reaction of the other side (your negotiating partner). There is a need to display empathy – to put yourself in the other person's shoes.

You are not negotiating in a vacuum. You have to work out an agreement with other people, who have their own objectives, problems and emotions! Here are some of the things to consider:

■ **Priorities.** What's important to them is what has the most value to them. So it is important to be aware of their likely gap between 'Desirable' and 'Worst'. You can't be sure of this until the discussion stage, but you can think about relative importance as they will see it.

> **case study** A buyer is negotiating the purchase of a batch of components for a machine. The buyer's position is as follows: 'Best' price £6.44 each; 'Worst" price £7.37. The seller's position is: 'Best' price £7.80 each; 'Worst" price £6.80. Here the negotiating issue is price. Somewhere between 'Desirable' and 'Worst'

# "If you are to put on another man's shoes you must first take off your own" Mark Twain, American author

■ **Wants.** You need to consider 'wants'. What they want and what you want. 'Wants' are crucial in any negotiation because you trade/exchange what they want with something that you have.

■ **Monkeys.** Does the other party have any serious 'monkeys on their back' – things that restrict their ability to move and to be flexible? If they have, you need to understand this, bring it into the open, and help them understand why this is a barrier to both. (I often find companies make credit terms non-negotiable. This can be a real obstacle to agreement, and movement on this issue need not be expensive.)

■ **Behaviour.** On every aspect of the negotiation keep asking yourself "How should I behave?" and "How will they behave?" Only then, for example, can you make a good decision about whether your 'Desirable' package is the appropriate place to start. And only then will you be ready for their 'Desirable' package.

## When you prepare, put yourself in the other party's shoes as well as considering your own position.

limits is a potential negotiated settlement for both parties. The area of overlap is a price between £6.80 and £7.37. If there is no overlap on another issue (say, payment terms) there would be a potential disagreement and failure to agree. This will only be overcome by one or both parties being flexible.

# 2.3

# Use a framework to guide you

From your preparation in 2.1 you have a framework which tells you how many variables you have – how many items there are on which you can give and take. You have an idea of what are the most important items to you and to the other party.

Use your framework throughout the negotiation, to allow you to control the result. Here are some of the ways you can do this:

**1** Focus early discussions on the variables you are more likely to agree on. This sets a constructive tone, but does not mean you agree on one or two items – see 4.5 'Don't get salami-ed'.

**case study** I helped in a negotiation that involved providing consignment stocks of fans for a customer building air-conditioning units (consignment stocks are buffer stocks, usually held on a customer's premises, but only invoiced when the customer draws the stock out). On the face of it, the variables on which we could give and take were the number of items, the quantity,

**2** You have identified the most valuable variables. Use this framework to calculate the value of any concession that you might be about to make.

**3** Use the framework to assess the cost of concessions on one variable with the cost of concessions in another area.

**4** Use your framework to decide whether you will hold back discussion on any of your variables. In other words, hold back on one item and use it as one of your final cards when you are wanting to come together and agree.

**5** When you negotiate, be prepared to use this framework to re-assess what variables are most important to your negotiating partner. Remember, you want to do repeat business with them.

**6** Be ready to use your framework to assess the value of any new variable that crops up in the negotiating process.

## Don't leave your preparation at home! Build on your prepared framework throughout the negotiation.

the price and payment terms. The more we prepared, however, the more variables we identified – the period of the agreement, obsolete stock/write off arrangements, carriage, currency changes, insurance costs, ownership of goods, and how to control damage. We considered the value of each of these variables, and this allowed us to negotiate with confidence.

# 2.4

# Decide on the most important issues

We have already considered the importance of preparation and using that preparation to carry you to a successful conclusion. You now need to be absolutely clear about what is important both to you and to the other party.

The case study below illustrates how the importance of an issue can be assessed – and re-assessed. The crux of the negotiation is the realization that a 'principle' that at first seems so important that it is non-negotiable turns out to be nothing of the kind.

**case study** A UK-based supplier of weighing machines wanted to expand into France with a new system targeted at bakeries. They were in discussion with an agent who wanted exclusive rights to sell the product into the French market. This exclusivity was very important to the agent. Unfortunately, the chairman of the UK company always refused to consider giving exclusive rights to anybody on

**"Only free men can negotiate; prisoners cannot enter into contracts. Your freedom and mine cannot be separated"** **Nelson Mandela, when in prison**

Here are some general principles that you should consider when weighing up the importance of the issues involved in a negotiation:

■ What's important to you might not be important to them.
■ What's important to them might not be important to you.
■ Before and during any negotiation you need to put yourself in the other person's shoes if you are to stand the best chance of reaching a win-win outcome. Consider the best location, timing and environment.
■ If something is clearly important to the other side, you need to realize that it's important to you too because it could help you reach agreement with them.

---

## Recognize what is most important to both parties, because that's what will dictate the course of the negotiation.

anything. To him it was a principle. The UK company was not geared up to sell to French bakeries, so there was a stalemate. Through the sales manager, common sense prevailed. The chairman was persuaded that what was 'important' to him was not important at all. The agent was given exclusivity for three years based on delivering a certain amount of business, and both parties benefited from the relationship.

# 2.5

# Know your team roles

Sometimes you will negotiate one-on-one, and sometimes you will negotiate as a team. If you are part of a team you all need to be quite clear which roles you each play – otherwise confusion will cost you dear. It will definitely cost you money, and it could cost you an agreement.

Mark McCormack who founded IMG – the global PR empire that manages the promotion of many of the world's leading sportsmen – favoured negotiating one-on-one. He felt that too often if the other team involved more than one negotiator, their egos got in the way and that made agreement more difficult. He has a point, and he was the boss, and he was a good one-on-one negotiator.

I am bound to say that there is another side to this argument. If two teams are properly prepared, and stick to their agreed roles, then good leading, summarizing and observing can increase the chances of success. Many times I have seen teams of three or more work well together to give each other time to think, and to invent creative options that have broken a deadlock and led to agreement.

So, what are the roles in a negotiating team?

### Leader
■ Not necessarily the most senior person.
■ Conducts the negotiation.
■ Trades concessions, makes proposals, calls for adjournment.
■ Only the leader knows what's next up their sleeve, so only the leader should lead!

### Summarizer
■ Summarizes periodically.
■ Asks questions to clarify points missed.
■ Asks questions to clarify matters of doubt.
■ Buys time for the leader.
■ Never takes over the leadership.

### Observer
■ Watches, listens and records.
■ Reads the negotiation.
■ Speaks only at adjournments.
■ Can provide the objective view.

If you are negotiating solo, in a one-on-one situation, you are fulfilling all three roles, but you do not fulfil them all at the same time! It is important that you realize when you are leading, when you are summarizing, and when you almost step back from the negotiation to see the bigger picture and take an objective view of what is going on.

## Make up your mind if your team is to be bigger than one, and if it is, be sure to stick to your roles.

# 2.6

# Plan your tactics

You have thought about the negotiation you are about to engage in – from your point of view, and through the eyes of the other party. The final part of your preparation is to consider your tactics.

You have plenty of ideas, but how will you use them to give you control over the negotiation? Here are a few tips:

**1** Decide whether you should be sharp and business-like, or relaxed and informal. Have your polite, opening questions ready, such as "How's business?" or "How's the family?"

**2** Decide whether you will start with something on which you can agree, or whether you will start on a difficult issue.

> **case study** I negotiated many times with Fred, a major purchaser of aluminium. He kept his cards close to his chest, liked to take his time and had real difficulty making decisions (in case they were wrong). He usually negotiated in a team of three. My tactics were always to take our time – four to six hours was the norm; make him feel comfortable in front of his colleagues,

# "Time spent on reconnaissance is never wasted" Duke of Wellington, British general

**3** How will you use the negotiating variables you have identified? Which ones will you start discussing? Which will most likely be in your first package? Which will you keep up your sleeve?

**4** Decide how long you think the discussion phase might take. Then pace your concessions accordingly.

**5** Who will go first? Fred (see the case study, below) always liked me to put my thoughts 'on the table' first.

How will you play it? Usually it's easy – your negotiating partner will provide the answer. If they like a long discussion, go for a long discussion. If they like to talk about their family, start with the family. There are limits to this, and you need to decide when to move on. You might be curious to know what the other party's view is of something. You could write to them, and have the answer before you meet.

## Use your knowledge of the other party to decide on the right tactics to employ.

and never present him with outrageous surprises. On some occasions, I wrote to him beforehand asking for his views on prices, volumes, and the likely split of materials. His response gave him a chance to think about it beforehand, and gave me useful information that allowed me to refine my tactics – which included taking my MD along for support.

# Discuss your respective positions

**It's time to meet.** With the initial pleasantries over, both parties need to state their opening positions and understand where the other is coming from. This chapter goes on to cover questioning skills, listening, using numbers that suit your case and the constant need to re-assess your position. Discussing each other's hopes and expectations sets the tone for the negotiation. Mutual understanding is the basis that should lead eventually to a satisfactory agreement.

# 3.1

# Let both parties set the scene

The preparation is over, and the negotiation starts with the discussion stage. This phase is crucial if the later bargaining stages are to result in agreement.

The Secrets to getting the best out of the discussion stage are:

**1** Develop a relaxed atmosphere by an exchange of small talk and pleasantries to suit the situation.

**2** Move on to the discussion of the factors that will be important. These are the background things to the negotiating variables. Not a proposition – just the background.

**case study** The importance of the discussion stage was shown by a negotiation I had with the MD and the HR director of a large German-owned UK company. I knew the MD to be a difficult person to deal with – cautious and revealing little. We were considering a contract covering a system for appraisal and performance management, plus management on an

**3** Clarify the position of both parties, generating an atmosphere of trust and confidence. If you can, find out what they think before you offer your view – because you can then modify your view if necessary.

**4** Ask questions so that you can establish what the other party's 'wants' are, and what their attitude is to the negotiation. You need to gather as much information as possible about their objectives, their commitment, their fears, their priorities.

**5** Listen more than you talk. Don't interrupt. That way you get the priceless information that will give you control over the agreement.

**6** Identify common ground and potential areas of difference, but just probe. Never let discussion degenerate into destructive argument that might take a long time to recover from.

**7** Summarize the discussion. Don't think of making a proposal until you have established what their shopping list is – that is their negotiating variables.

## Get the discussion stage right: it sets the tone for the whole negotiation.

outsourced basis of the resultant management development and sales training. At the end of a wide-ranging debate about philosophy, approach and detail, the MD turned to the HR director and said "I've seen a side to David Brown that I've never seen before." We'd had a great discussion. I knew that I had the business before we had even exchanged proposals!

# 3.2

# Understand the other party's viewpoint

We have stressed the importance of seeing things through the eyes of the other party. You don't reach agreement on your own – you can only reach it with another party. So let's look at successful ways of working with and through other people.

These tips are not just about successful negotiating – they are about successful leadership, management, buying, selling, in fact successful anything that involves working with other people.

■ **Empathy.** Know what empathy is. It can be defined as an ability to see things through someone else's eyes. Alternatively, it is about entering someone else's world. Be them. Check that the timing and the environment are right for both of you.

"Successful people influence emotions – not just thought"

**John Kotter, Harvard Business School professor**

**one minute wonder** Don't get hung up on logic and rational thinking. We need to accept that people's feelings will often cause them to do illogical things. To reach agreement with them we need to let them run with their feelings and use their feelings to move towards an agreement.

■ **Emotions.** Understand the importance of emotions. John Kotter in *The Heart of Change* explains that we usually expect people to make decisions based on logic. Unfortunately, he says people often make decisions based on emotion. We should allow for this and take this into account in our negotiations.

■ **Feelings.** 'Listen' to your feelings. Another way of looking at Kotter's ideas is to say that normally we look at task, then process, and maybe feelings last. The behaviour of your negotiating partner is often driven by feelings, so try looking at feelings first, process second and the job last. Feelings are like facts; they are important.

■ **Interests.** Discover and explore mutual interests. Explore things that are important to both of you if you are to reach agreement.

# Recognize that your feelings and the feelings of the other party are as important as logic.

# 3.3

# Clearly state your opening position

You've had the discussion. You've both talked around the various items in each of your shopping baskets, and why they are important. Now it is important to give an executive summary of what is important to you. This clearly shows your negotiating partner where you are coming from. It isn't yet a proposal but it is a helicopter view that will put the negotiation on the right track.

What's in your opening position will depend on your objectives, your negotiating partner's objectives, and the discussion you have just had. Here are just a few examples of what you might include in your

**case study** A few months into his presidency, US President Barack Obama embarked on negotiations that are important to all of us, none more so than those with Palestinian President Mahmoud Abbas and Israeli Prime Minister Benjamin Netanyahu. Many had tried to broker peace before him, but Obama made a fresh start

opening position if you are a buyer or a seller. You could say most or all of the seven things below as you set the scene with your opening position! These are not proposals or packages, but they tell the other party where you are coming from. If you express this clearly, it will help them understand your first package when you come to present it.

- "I want to protect our good relationship."
- "I must be mindful of the need to protect our margins."
- "I want to agree things today that will allow both of us to be successful this year."
- "I am looking to support your new initiative into the Indian market."
- "I must be aware of the need to agree something today that will not disrupt the market place in which we both operate."
- "I must buy competitively enough to allow our sales people to sell this product."
- "I must agree a specification with you which allows my fellow buyers to buy from alternative sources."

# State your opening position clearly in terms of what you want to finish up with.

by clearly defining his opening position. He said, "The Palestinians have a right to a state of their own, and the Israelis have a right to exist as a state. Also, building settlements on the West Bank must stop." There is still a long way to go – but let us hope that a negotiated peace will result.

# 3.4

# Ask plenty of questions

Asking the right questions is the key to unlocking a negotiation and understanding everything you need to know in order to reach agreement.

The Kipling quote (right) is probably the most used quotation in management training, sales training and negotiation training. Kipling was a journalist before he became an author and poet. He is saying that asking questions gave him the knowledge to be good at his job. Let's look at the basics of asking good questions, and some practical examples of how to ask them.

■ **Ask open questions.** Open questions persuade people to talk, and give you the information you need. "What is the most important thing to you?" is likely to give you much more than "Is that important?"

**case study** Here's a case study with a difference. Next time you see an interview on TV or hear one on the radio, notice how the interviewer who gets results will not ask multiple questions or ask too many closed questions. Closed questions can easily bring the

> "I kept six honest serving men, they taught me all I knew. Their names are What and Why and When and How and Where and Who"

**Rudyard Kipling, British poet and novelist**

■ **Ask one question at a time.** Avoid multiple questions. If you ask more than one question at a time, the other party becomes confused, and you don't know which question they are answering. "How do you feel about that? Does it appeal to you?" is likely to lead to a "yes" or "no" answer. It is best to ask just one question, then listen to the reply.

■ **When to ask closed questions.** Use closed questions to check on progress or to check whether you are both agreed. "Would you agree with me?" could well result in a straight "yes" or "no", but you know where you stand, and what question to ask next. "Why?" might be your next question – if you really want to understand the answer you've been given. In other words, the 'why' could be more revealing than the answer to your first question.

## Good questions help you to understand what you have to do to reach agreement.

interview to an uncomfortable halt. The skilled interviewer will draw out the interviewee with open questions, and elicit the interesting information that we need. You need to do the same in the course of your negotiations and in your business life in general!

# 3.5

# Listen more than you talk

Listening is a crucial skill. There is no point in asking a great question that could give you priceless information, if you don't listen to the answer.

There are two stages to good listening. First, you have to hear the words. Secondly, you have to understand what is meant by the words. The first stage is not listening, it's hearing. The second stage is about developing a mutual understanding. Good listening leads to agreements, and here are a few tips to improve your listening:

■ **Ensure the environment allows you to listen effectively.** Make sure the room isn't stuffy or noisy.

**case study** I was once asked to facilitate a discussion between two people who were not working well together, and who both felt that a third party could help them broker a peace. Very quickly, it seemed to me that there were barriers to listening that would prevent us from making progress that day. Barrier number one was attitudinal – the manager concerned

# "You've got two ears and one mouth. Use them in that proportion" German proverb

■ **Have empathy.** Understand what is being said. Look behind the words used by your negotiating partner.

■ **Concentrate.** Prepare; then avoid distractions to avoid missing anything. Take notes. Make gestures to show that you are listening – nod your head, make eye contact, smile, frown, lean forward.

■ **Watch for signals that will help you.** A change of voice tone, pauses, stutters, eye movement and facial expressions.

■ **Keep an open mind.** Get rid of your prejudices or any bias that will stop you listening.

■ **Let them finish.** Don't interrupt.

■ **Cool down to listen.** Avoid face-to-face meetings or telephone calls when you are angry.

■ **The power of silence.** Never forget the power of a pause.

Most of the above are to do with your attitude and your approach to listening.

## If you want to be a successful negotiator, first be a good listener.

had his mind on other things (which I knew about, but the other person didn't.) Barrier number two was environmental – there was noisy building work going on above us. We agreed to move to a better time and a better place. Real listening began, and the relationship improved to a level that allowed the two people to work together.

# 3.6

# Re-assess your tactics

Where have we got to in our study of negotiating? We've prepared thoroughly. We have clear objectives. We've had a discussion that results in each party understanding where the other is coming from. The next step is to re-assess your tactics in the light of what you have learnt so far.

During the discussion phase you need to:

**1** Check what new negotiating variables have cropped up, and put your Desirable/Probable/Worst values on them.

**"The wise adapt themselves to circumstances, as water moulds itself to the pitcher" Chinese proverb**

**one minute wonder** Never assume anything. If you look at what ASSUME spells out, it is that it makes an ASS out of U and ME. So don't assume, constantly re-assess your tactics from the start to the finish of any negotiation.

**2** Re-assess which are the most valuable negotiating variables to you, including the new ones that have appeared.

**3** Assess the importance of each negotiating variable to the other party. Is their shopping list of variables the same as yours?

**4** If you have chosen to keep one or two negotiating variables 'up your sleeve' for later use, ask yourself, "Does this still make sense?" Would it be a good move to change your priorities in view of the new variables that have come to light?

**5** Do all of the above by using skilled questions and carefully listening to the answers.

# In your initial discussions be prepared to review your tactics to account for any new variables that arise.

# 3.7

# Use numbers that suit your case

Numbers are very powerful when used to support your case. They can tip the other party towards agreeing when up to that point they were hesitating.

The case study that I am sharing with you here is about a situation in which I did more than use numbers in a 'funny' way. I lied to someone that I have known for 30 years, and they found out. Happily they forgave me, and I vowed never to do it again to anyone. I'm not suggesting that you should lie, but you can use numbers in a way that suits your case. I call them 'funny numbers' because they are misleading, but 'funny numbers' can seriously influence any negotiation. Here are a few examples of funny numbers.

**case study** Graham was a huge buyer of aluminium. He was in direct competition with our largest customer, with whom we had already agreed a price increase. We were negotiating what increase Graham would accept, and in the course of the negotiation, he asked, "Have you agreed a price increase of more than 5% with our competitor?" To my shame, I said, "Yes", which

# "There are lies, damned lies, and statistics" **Countless politicians since 1894**

■ As a buyer of garments you could say, "You expect me to pay £7.20 each for those!" It would be more powerful to say, "Look, I'm spending half a million pounds with you each year on garments, and I expect a good price!"

■ If you want to be known as the biggest producer in town, then pick the measure that allows you to say that. Whether it's turnover, people employed or square metres of floor space, the message will be, "We're the biggest operator in town."

■ A buyer could remind you that he spends £150,000 per year with you. If you want to counter that you could re-present it as £400 per day, or say, "That just puts you in our top ten customers."

■ Government ministers will use figures to suit their case. They might say inflation is 4.6%, but if they want people to see a lower figure, they will exclude special items like oil and housing costs which have gone up due to global events, and say it's 2.1%.

## Use numbers creatively to back up your arguments.

was untrue. But there was no need to lie! I should have told part of the truth, or I could have used a 'funny' number. I could have said "Their increase is more than 5% on products that you take" (which was true, but not across the board). I could have said "The increase was more than inflation". At the time inflation was 4.3%, so my response would have been true.

# 3.8

# Consider cost, price and value

If you are to reach agreement with someone, you will offer things that they value. This Secret is about knowing the difference between value, cost and price.

We've looked at a negotiation framework that involves each party having a shopping list of negotiating variables. In the early stages, these two lists will not contain the same things. At agreement they will contain the same things. And agreement will have been reached because each party sees real value in each of the negotiating variables. Let's consider some definitions, and then look at how value is important.

**case study** A large wholesaler shipped its goods out on pallets that cost them £4.50. They made thousands of pallets, and tried to negotiate an arrangement with their customers that involved a fee of £5.50 for any pallets that were not returned. It cost them £3.20 to collect and recycle the pallets. So the gain to the supplier of getting their pallets back was a miserable £1.30, with a proportion of the pallets damaged. One customer saw things differently. They needed pallets

# "Price is what you pay. Value is what you get"

**Warren Buffett, American investor and businessman**

■ **Cost.** Cost is just that. If a company buys a car for £10,000 the cost is £10,000. If a company has a system for measuring cost, it can identify the cost of anything.

■ **Price.** This too is straightforward. It's how much an item is purchased for or sold at.

■ **Value.** This is more complex, and the one you need to work with if you are to be an effective negotiator. Value is in the eye of the beholder. Value is perceived. A buyer perceives that something is valuable or not valuable. If your negotiating variables contain lots of items that the buyer perceives to be valuable to them, then your chances of reaching agreement will shoot up.

## Assess the value of everything through the eyes of the other party.

to ship their goods on, and could sell any surplus pallets locally. Being small, they had no pallet making facility and would have had to pay £8.30 for pallets. The wholesaler saw sense. They conceded the £5.50 charge and the customer had free pallets that were of real value (£8.30) to them. Charging for pallets did nothing for the wholesaler, and making this concession provided real value in the eyes of the customer and allowed them to agree in other areas.

# 3.9

# Summarize before any proposal

Before you make your first proposal, you need to summarize where both parties have come from, and their present position. This allows your first proposal to be well received.

The Secret here is to present your case in a persuasive way. Your summary should leave the other party in no doubt that one way or another it is in their interests for the two sides to reach agreement. Here are some useful points to help persuade them of this in your summary.

**1** Put your negotiation into context. Summarize, for example, why it is important to both of you to reach agreement in the short term or long term and why it is important in the market place that you both operate in.

**2** Remind your partner what is important to them, and what is important to you.

**one minute wonder** In negotiating, as in any business discussion, it is crucial to make sure things are seen in context. It's useless making what you think is a fabulous point if the person you are communicating with fails to see it. There is a constant need to help them see the big picture if you are to persuade them on a single issue.

**3** Touch on some of the things that you will have to agree on (the variables) in order to reach agreement – but keep one or two up your sleeve.

**4** Use plenty of words that will bring you together, like 'we', 'us', 'jointly', 'together'. Remember, you are not dealing with an 'opponent' – you are partners in a negotiation that you both need to agree upon.

**5** Recognize that such a summary might be usefully repeated at future points in the negotiation. It could allow you both to remember what is important, and give you time to come up with creative ideas.

# If you want to engage with the other party, summarize before starting to make proposals and bargain.

# Deal only in packages

**You are now in a position** to make proposals to each other. This chapter explains how the basis of all offers needs to be a package – not just one item but a collection of items that we will call a package. We will look at why the other party should offer the first package, and about making your first package credible. There are tips on how to persuade the other party by offering them choices, how to use persuasive language, and how to know when you need to adjourn.

# 4.1

# Packages must be easy to understand

If you present packages that are clearly spelled out, you can trade with those packages. You can give on some items and take on others. It is important not to get sucked into agreeing on any single item, even though you may have discussed it for some time. This is true of any variable.

If you agree one item at a time, that leaves you with nothing to give and take on. It is known as being 'salami-ed'. In 4.5 I will explore the concept in greater detail. Here are some important aspects of swapping proposals in the form of packages.

**1** They allow you to clearly state what you are offering, and for the other party to check what you mean by your proposal.

**2** They allow your negotiating partner to do the same for you – to spell out clearly what they are proposing.

**3** The simpler and quicker the proposal the better. In the case study in 4.3 Derek presents a package of five items. He proposes quickly: "We can offer you a three-month deal, with the specification defined, in a minimum quantity of one tonne per batch, and if you take 50 tonnes we can keep the price increase to 6.3%." Say it out loud! It takes only a few seconds.

**4** A proposal is not an offer. It is an offer with a condition or conditions. In Derek's example above the condition is "if you take 50 tonnes, and if you accept the whole package".

**5** Keep it simple. The simpler you make your packages the less room there is for misunderstanding and the more likely agreement is. Think of KISS – Keep It Simple Stupid.

**6** Properly presented packages clearly show any differences between the two sides. This is not a problem! It shows what movement is necessary in order to reach agreement.

**7** Remember, you can still keep negotiating variables up your sleeve. You don't have to put them all on the table at once. If you have a few up your sleeve it makes sense to drip feed them, and save the clincher to the end.

# Propose packages, not single items, and always attach a condition or conditions to every offer.

# 4.2

# Let them offer the first package

You've done your preparation to the best of your ability, and you've had a healthy discussion, but you can't be sure of the other party's starting point. Unless they do the starting!

There are many reasons why it is important for the other side to declare what they are looking for first.

**1** You may be pleasantly surprised by the fact that their first package contains things that are better than the best you have

**case study** My sales team was negotiating aluminium supplies with a producer of high-pressure beer barrels. There were lots of negotiating variables, including volume, batch size, time scales, the specification, and of course price. Derek and I had prepared together, with Derek to take the lead and me acting as summarizer and observer. Their buyer was an authority on aluminium and future prices – this accounted for a massive proportion of their costs. We had imagined

imagined in your preparation. If you make the first proposal, you will never get the chance to find this out.

**2** You will now be full of confidence and optimism, because reaching agreement will be easier than you had imagined.

**3** You will know from their first proposal what your partner's key issues are (unless they are being very clever and keeping this up their sleeve).

**4** You might receive a shock if the other party offers the first package, and it is a very aggressive one. However, if they are going to be aggressive, the quicker you realize it the better.

**5** You have more flexibility if the other party 'bats first'. You can adjust your proposals in tune with theirs.

# If you want control be sure to let the other party make the first proposal.

that the 'Desirable' result for us on price was an increase of 4.3%, and the worst case was no increase at all. Imagine our surprise when their opening package contained amongst other things a price rise to us (cost increase to them) of 5%. Derek then asked for an adjournment. We revised our 'Desirable', 'Probable' and 'Worst' framework and went on to reach agreement with a happy buyer and happy sellers – truly a win-win situation.

# 4.3

# Make your first package challenging but credible

Making your first package challenging is important because if you don't do this you will never know how much money you have left on the table – never know what you could have achieved.

The most important thing about your first package is that it should be a package! It should not be just an offer of price, or if you are a buyer it should not just be a commitment to take a particular volume. Your first package should contain at least two variables on which you are prepared to give and take. Make sure it is all these things:

**case study** In 4.2 I told you how Derek and I succeeded in getting the buyer to propose the first package. We adjourned to re-plan our Desirable, Probable and Worst. When we resumed, Derek presented a package that included the volume that we expected, batch sizes, the specification, a three-month time scale, and a price increase of 6.3% – confidently

**■ Challenging.** It should be bold enough to show that you are serious, and give you a chance to realize your 'Desirable' objectives.

**■ Desirable.** You decided on this when you prepared. The discussion may have prompted you to modify your 'Desirable' – to be more ambitious or less. Start with your current view of your Desirable.

**■ Credible.** If your first proposal is ridiculously aggressive, the other side may react badly and may take a long time to revert to being reasonable. A credible first package sets the tone for the whole negotiation. Note: If the other party's offer is not credible, don't panic. The answers are to be found in the rest of this book. The best response is to laugh or flinch or start to leave the room (see 6.5). Explain that their ridiculous start has undermined their credibility in your eyes. Ask them to make a more serious proposal, and remember that you are not going to split anything 50/50 (see 5.5). If you negotiate in a structured way, their ridiculous demands will not adversely affect your position.

**■ Assertive.** Your negotiating partner needs to feel that your behaviour is neither submissive (in which case they might take advantage of you) nor aggressive (in which case they might become difficult). Your behaviour needs to be appropriate, that is to say assertive.

# Be bold but credible when you propose your first package.

asking for a full 2% higher than our early preparation had led us to expect. We couldn't settle for their 5%. If we had, they would almost certainly feel that they had 'lost'. The buyer rejected our package, but it was credible enough for the negotiation to stay on course, and presented with enough confidence for the buyer to take it seriously.

# 4.4

# Be confident with your opening package

Presenting your opening package with confidence is crucial to the rest of the negotiating session. It sets the right tone. Let's have a look at how a confident start is likely to lead to a confident finish, or conversely how a nervous start will lead to more nerves. Confidence is important because it's like so many other things. It's infectious.

If you start timidly and then become aggressive, you will be confused and so will your negotiating partner. The result will be uncertainty and lack of agreement. Start assertively. Similarly, if you start as if the other party were your best friend, and then switch to being incredibly business-like, confusion will result. Your behaviour needs to be consistent unless you deliberately change it to create a particular effect.

If you are confident with your opening package you will feel confident going forward. Your partner will know what's going on, they will sense why, and they will open up and be confident. Success breeds success. All this is only true if you are confident – not aggressive or arrogant, and not timid. Be assertive!

# "No one can make you feel inferior without your consent"

**Eleanor Roosevelt, wife of US president Franklin D. Roosevelt**

There is a case for quickly changing your behaviour in some situations, but not when presenting your opening package. The best time to spring a surprise on the other party is if you are trying to change the course of the negotiation – for instance, when you decide to introduce a new variable, or when you seek to clinch agreement.

Here are some of the things that you can do to boost your confidence when negotiating one on one or as part of a team:

■ Understand the strengths and weaknesses of both parties. (See Secret 6.3.)
■ Keep telling yourself that you are OK.
■ Be clear about what you are trying to do with your life, your business life, and your future relationship with your negotiating partner - not just what success in this negotiation will look like.
■ Visualize yourself being successful. Eventually you will believe it.
■ Be clear about what your boss or team members expect you to achieve.
■ Be clear about the point at which you will walk away without agreement.
■ Don't plough on if you are feeling uneasy. Ask for an adjournment.
■ If you sense the other party is feeling uneasy or lacking in confidence, once again you could consider an adjournment. To ram home your 'advantage' may not be a good idea.

## Present your package assertively but not aggressively.

# 4.5

# Don't get 'salami-ed'

You will find this colourful expression in most modern books on negotiating. It describes the process of allowing your negotiating partner to cut up the negotiating package into a series of individual items – like thin slices of salami – and then your agreeing to them one by one.

If you agree individual items one at a time, then when the other party suddenly raises another important item, you have nothing left to bargain with. You cannot give and take, because you've agreed all the other bits already. To avoid being 'salami-ed' in this way, think packages when you prepare, discuss packages when you start, bargain packages rather than argue over one item, and finally agree one complete package.

**case study** The Hungarian communist leader Mátyás Rákosi considered what Stalin did in Europe in 1945 to 1949 to be 'slicing salami'. After World War II, Stalin and the Soviet Union gradually gained control of Albania, Bulgaria, Poland, Romania, Hungary, Czechoslovakia and finally East Germany. He saw this as protecting the USSR from future attack. The Western Allies saw it as

Here are some useful tips on how to avoid being salami-ed:

**1** Discuss single items by all means, but only present and bargain with packages.

**2** Ask the other party, "Is there anything else that we need to discuss in your package before we move on?" Or, "What else do we need to look at before we reach agreement?"

**3** Use "if" as you move to bargain. Say, "If you do (a) and (b) and (c) then I will give you this…"

**4** Don't let the other party chop up the negotiation into a series of smaller negotiations. You might try this yourself, but don't let them get away with it.

**5** Constantly see each negotiating variable in the context of the whole negotiation.

**6** Be aware of the relative value of each of the negotiating variables (the component parts of the negotiation).

## Always deal in packages. If you don't you may be cornered with nowhere to go.

empire building – but they could do little about it because it was done bit by bit. No single thing that Stalin did was worth going to war over, so Stalin's tactics achieved what he wanted. It was not until 40 years later, with the fall of the Berlin Wall, that the tide was reversed. Don't wait years to recover from poor negotiating tactics – avoid being salami-ed.

# 4.6

# Know when to adjourn

Knowing when to adjourn (take a break) is important to both parties in a negotiation because if either of you is pushed into doing something when you are not ready, it will have a negative effect on the outcome. When you need time to think, ask for an adjournment.

In my experience, people do not take enough breaks in negotiations, and this hinders agreement and leaves a sense of dissatisfaction. Let's remind ourselves of the sort of negotiation that we are looking at in this book. We are not looking at a one-off transaction – if you are, then get away with whatever your conscience will allow. We are dealing with people with whom we want a relationship, who will come back and do business with us again and again. If you or your partner is feeling really uncomfortable, take an adjournment to allow you to collect your thoughts. Here are a few tips that will help you decide when to adjourn:

■ If you are negotiating one on one (or if you are one negotiating with more than one) be aware of when you need time to think around a point – particularly a new point that has been raised by the other party.
■ When you are part of a team, be prepared for any of the team to ask for an adjournment. This is much better than a team member coming out publicly with something that is unhelpful to the leader or the team.
■ In political or industrial relations negotiations, adjourning for weeks

or days are often necessary for both parties to digest lots of information, and to allow consultation with other stakeholders.

■ Don't adjourn – even for a few minutes – if you feel that valuable momentum will be lost.

■ Take a break when the exchange seems to be stuck in a circular argument. Give both parties time to create offers that will break the deadlock. To allow people to take stock, you could say, "I feel we are going nowhere here. I feel we are scoring points off each other, and I think we should both reflect on what we are trying to achieve."

■ One way for you to take a brief, no fuss adjournment is to visit the toilet, and think.

■ Be aware that our ability to concentrate has limits. Lack of concentration means poor listening, and poor listening is dangerous! When you feel that limit is reached, take a break.

■ Any time you need to re-assess your Desirable/Probable/Worst objectives, you should consider adjourning.

■ Remember that any adjournment creates an expectation that new proposals or a new approach will be presented.

How to take adjournments is also well worth considering:

      ■ Summarize before you break.
      ■ Withdraw to a private area.
      ■ Invite the other party to consider one or two issues.
      ■ Agree when and on what basis the meeting will re-convene.

## Use adjournments to suit the situation, and to encourage agreement.

# 4.7

# Give the other party a choice

We all love choices, and usually react badly if we are told to "take it or leave it". Saying this can seriously reduce the chances of a negotiation being successful.

Don't leave the other party with no choice unless you really have reached deadlock and you are happy for them to reject what you are offering. There are times when it is an appropriate tactic (see below), but there are usually better options that will stop you getting boxed in and keep the negotiation open.

**1** **Trade packages.** Packages of two items or more keep the negotiation going. If you talk only about price you come to a grinding halt. If you talk about price and delivery you have the simplest package of all. If you offer a package that contains price, quantity and delivery, then even if you say "that's the

**case study** For over 20 years General Electric in the USA used "take it or leave it" tactics in their labour negotiations. The company was careful to back their offer with impressive statistics that were difficult to argue with, and usually this worked. Then, one year, it

best I can do," the fact that you have presented a package means that discussion is likely to continue and agreement is still possible.

**2** **Have plenty of items in your package.** The more items you have in your package, the more flexible you can be, and the less likely you are to have to resort to take it or leave it.

"Take it or leave it" may work for you if:
■ You soften your language to something like "that's the best I can do".
■ You are exhausted and want to bring things to a head.
■ Your customers are used to that sort of language and behaviour.
■ A drop in price to one customer would cost you a fortune elsewhere in your market or your resulting margins would become unacceptably low.
■ You are prepared for the loss of face that comes with failure to agree. This could be with the other party, within your industry, or with your boss.
■ You can justify your stance with an undeniable fact.

# Until you run out of options, keep trading packages.

didn't. The electrical workers decided to "leave it", and what followed was the costliest strike in US history. All the money that GE had saved was wiped out by union hostility to the company's highly confrontational "take it or leave it" approach.

# 4.8

# Show that you are flexible

If negotiation is a matter of give and take, then to negotiate successfully you must be flexible. If you say the word "if" as in "if you do this, then I will do that", you are suggesting that you will be flexible.

There is no point in saying that you understand the need to be flexible in a negotiation if you don't act in a flexible fashion. Flexible behaviour starts with a flexible attitude. When I help people develop, I ask them to focus on the important distinction between the need to change attitude, skill, or knowledge (ASK). The activity required to develop each of these three things is very different. It's easy to give you knowledge of flexibility – we are doing that here. You can practise the

**case study** I once knew a business owner who was a most belligerent individual. Douglas ran a profitable training and development business, but he ran it with a rod of iron. He was extremely inflexible. One of the things he had a fixation about was a rigid system for collecting money and controlling credit. He was quick to send solicitor's letters and quick to put programmes

skill of being flexible, but a flexible attitude needs to start inside your head! To be a flexible negotiator, you need to want to be flexible. So here are a few ideas that should increase your desire to be flexible.

**1** Your high-level strategy and objectives are more important than low-level, detailed tactics. Yet poor tactics can destroy the best strategies. Strategies and tactics need to fit together, and you need to adapt your approach.

**2** Tactics that work in a buyer's market may not work in periods of short supply.

**3** Tactics that worked well for you with someone yesterday may not work next week if their situation has changed. Re-assess your approach. Being flexible is a must.

**4** Ends do not always justify means. Presumably there are some things that you would not do even if it did help you achieve your goals (like lie!) You have to make judgements about what is acceptable to you and to your negotiating partner. What is acceptable in one situation may not be acceptable in another.

## Continually re-assess your approach according to the situation.

on stop. This worked well until a competitor (a former employee) offered a distinctly similar service. Then he started to lose business. The customers who resented his heavy-handed approach had long memories – and they now had somewhere else to go. If Douglas had been prepared to be more flexible his good business would have suffered less.

# 4.9

# Tailor your language

There is no point in patting yourself on the back, and being pleased with your message. Pat yourself on the back if your message is well received by your audience and achieves the result that you want!

I increasingly use neuro-linguistic programming (NLP) in coaching people not just in negotiating, but also in selling, presenting, and interviewing. The basis of NLP is how we prefer to receive information. We all receive communications through three very different routes: the audio route – by hearing; the visual route – by seeing; and the feelings route – by appeals to our emotions (we touched on this in 3.2). We all use all of these three senses to receive messages, but we all have a preference for one of the three. When presenting your case at any stage in a negotiation, there is always a danger that you use your own

**case study** I once recorded a coaching session in which people were working in pairs on an exercise designed to practise negotiating skills. The two parties had got the message about packages, and then one said, "I think I could probably stretch to approximately 1,500 units if you could maybe change the price to something around £5 and if you can ease the payment

preferred means of communication. You should try to appeal to all three senses, but above all to the sense preferred by your audience.

Try to understand the other party's preferred method of receiving messages, and use it. If the person with whom you are negotiating uses words like "I heard you say…" (audio) or "I see that…" (visual) or "I feel that…" (feelings), then take the hint and use the same language.

Here are a few further important tips on how to appeal to people, how to persuade them, and how to get your message across:

■ **Don't use round numbers.** Round numbers give the impression that there is plenty of room to negotiate. So make your first offer £1,115 and not £1,000. £1,115 sounds much more serious and considered.

■ **Don't use floppies.** This means don't use feeble words like "might" because they undermine your case. Use words like "will".

■ **Don't just tell people.** If possible tell them, show them something to support the idea, and let them touch it. We do this when we hand someone a document or some other visual aid. Research shows that people are twice as likely to retain information that they see rather than just hear, and four times more likely to retain information that they hear, see and touch.

# Make your message appeal to the person you are trying to influence.

terms." How many floppies can you count – on top of a hopeless round number? "Think", "probably", "stretch", "maybe", "something", "around", and "ease" could all be eliminated to good effect. That was seven words in one sentence that undermined his case! He could so easily have said "I will buy 1,500 units at £4.85 with 60 days credit."

# Bargain your way to success

**After exchanging packages** you have to bridge the gap between their package and yours. You will do this through movement as you bargain with each other. This chapter looks at how to manage concessions, the need to track them, and the importance of constantly bearing in mind your objectives before making concessions. Above all, I will emphasize how important the tiny word "if" is in the negotiating process, and how to use it to your advantage.

# 5.1

# Movement allows agreement

Negotiation is about compromise – give and take – so it follows that negotiation is about movement. We will look at the tactics of movement in this chapter, but first let's look at the big picture so that you can be sure of its importance.

Negotiations are about the movement of two parties from two opposing positions to a single position of mutual agreement. So, it follows that movement is the lifeblood of negotiations. You should be constantly re-assessing your approach to these three questions throughout every negotiation:

■ **How far apart are we?** That is, how far apart are we on each of the variables that are the basis of our negotiating framework?

■ **Where do we have to move?** Where do we have to get to in order to reach agreement? It is the point at which we will agree! It is Stephen Covey's "end" as in "start with the end in mind".

■ **What do I have to do?** You know how far apart you are; you now know where you will meet; finally you need to ask yourself, "What do I have to do to get there, what do I have to do to bridge the gap?"

Make constant use of your negotiating framework. On each of your variables ask yourself, "How far apart are we, where do we have to move to, and how do we bridge the gap?"

You and your partner need to send signals that you are both prepared to move, otherwise you will drift towards deadlock and failure to agree. Signals usually come in the form of a change of emphasis in a previously rigid statement. So, for instance, "never" becomes "maybe," "impossible" becomes "that could be difficult," and "no" becomes "not as things stand." Early on in the negotiation, these would be floppies (see 4.9), but when both parties are looking for movement, they are a signal that movement is possible. They are grounds for hope. Here is another example of an aspect of negotiating that is not clear cut, not black or white, but requiring you to have a feel for the situation and use your good sense.

When you feel that some movement is required, look for a signal. If you don't receive one, send a signal that will prompt movement from the other party. Questions are important in this situation, questions such as "Why are you so determined to stick on that point?" or "What's needed to bring us together?"

Signals are an essential part of negotiations because they indicate the possibility of movement without committing the negotiator to anything specific like a revised package. The revised package follows, and you are one step nearer agreement.

# In order to reach agreement, entice movement from the other party, and be prepared to move yourself.

# 5.2

# "If" is the biggest word in negotiating

We have already touched on the significance of the word "if" in Secret 4.1. Successful negotiators start proposals with "If you…". Remember this, put it into practise and you could save yourself a fortune.

It is essential to say, "If you do this, this and this, I will do that…" because you are attaching a condition to a proposal. You are making the point that this is a package and that the other party should either accept the package or reject the package and offer an alternative. What you are not doing is giving the other party the chance to accept bits of your

**case study** One of my consultant friends, Neil, was negotiating a spell as an interim industrial relations manager for a company going through a period of change. He was asked to reduce his daily rate by £20 per day to clinch agreement on a package that the MD of the company had spelled out. This covered all the variables they had been discussing, including a mileage allowance of 55 pence per mile. "OK," said Neil, "If you increase the mileage allowance to 62 pence per mile,

package, and reject other bits. If you allow the other party to accept the best bits of your package, and agree them in isolation, then you are being 'salami-ed' (see 4.5). You are getting into a situation where you could agree on several negotiating variables one after the other, only to be left with one variable on which you don't agree. You have been 'salami-ed', you have nowhere to go, and that could be expensive!

When you negotiate use a calculator. If you don't then you are either brilliant at mental arithmetic, or you are not negotiating in a structured way. Your package contains several negotiating variables, each of which has a different value to you. For each item you may move from 'Desirable' to 'Probable', even to 'Worst', as you make concessions. How do you know how valuable each concession is? Consider the case study in 4.2. The other party might ask you to reduce the price by one quarter of one percent. How do you know how valuable this is? How do you know how valuable it is in relation to the other items in the package? You need a calculator!

# Use "if" as the first word in every proposal you make.

providing we are agreed that it is six months' work; that I will work five days per week with me working remotely from my office on one of those days; that I will be paid weekly in arrears, and that all out of pocket expenses (hotels and meals) will be reimbursed at cost, I will reduce my daily rate by £10. Neil conceded £10 per day and worked out that the extra 7 pence per mile halved the cost of the concession to him. After more small adjustments they shook hands on the deal.

# 5.3

# If you concede, attach a condition

This principle is so important that I am devoting this section to a selection of practical examples that show how this can work for you. You can then come up with proposals that will suit your particular situation.

You may be any of the negotiating types that we considered in the introduction – buyer, seller, government officer, family member, industrial relations officer, or others. I am going to give examples for each, but please appreciate that these are only examples.

Some of them start "If you…", as discussed in 5.2, but some start with "If I do this… will you …? For me, the latter is too likely to result in someone saying "No". However, this approach is sometimes used, particularly in the closing stages of a negotiation when you are asking someone point blank, "Will you accept this?" The challenge for you is to come up with the right words to persuade the other party in the situation in which you are negotiating. Here are a few examples of what people might say when they are put in a difficult situation.

■ **In the family 1.** A wife wants her husband to take the children to school, but he is aware that he might have to do the shopping as well. So he concedes, "I'll take them to school, if you sort out the shopping."

**■ In the family 2.** Your son wants to behave just as he likes, wants an ice cream, and wants to play football with his friend. You concede, "If you help me today, we get ice creams and I will pick up Paul so that you can play football tomorrow?" Children (like some adults) are very persistent, and expect you to give in, so be aware of this when deciding how to respond to their demands.

**■ The buyer 1.** A buyer is under pressure to buy large batches of 1,500 units, at a price they don't like. They concede, "If you let me buy a minimum batch of 1,000, if you will supply them on a two-day lead time, and if you accept payment in 60 days, then we will accept your price of £5.23 each."

**■ The buyer 2.** A buyer is being asked to accept a package that is less favourable than they want to settle for. They concede, "If you give us first refusal on all your obsolete stock, I will accept the package that you have just offered."

**■ The seller.** A seller is being asked to reduce the price by 1%. They concede, "If you will commit to featuring our goods in the front of your catalogue, we will reduce the price by 0.75% and pay £1,000 towards your printing costs."

**■ The employer.** The employees know that they face a cut to a four-day week, and wish to maintain their existing hourly rates. So the employer concedes, "If you are prepared to accept a four-day week and a 2% reduction in the rate per hour, we will commit to no redundancies for at least six months."

I could go on, but the requirement is for you to be imaginative and structured in your own negotiations. Often, the concessions you will have to make will be wrapped up in a package that is more complex than the examples above, as in the case study in 5.2.

# Imaginative conditions can make any concession desirable.

# 5.4

# Make your first concession small

Making your first concession a small one – ideally on a relatively minor issue – sets the tone for the negotiation. This involves risk and uncertainty, so requires real courage. It is what Steve Gates means by "being comfortable with being uncomfortable".

In Secret 5.5 we will look at several ideas that will allow you to manage concessions effectively. Before we go there, I want to focus on the importance of starting small. Negotiating expert Chester Karrass has conducted extensive trials that have shown:

**1** People who start with small concessions get better results than people who start big. Those who make small concessions followed by even smaller concessions get the best results of all. The message is start small and get smaller.

**2** People who make their first concession on a major issue secure the worst results.

**3** People who make the biggest single concession in the course of a negotiation fare worst of all.

# "The key to negotiating is learning to be comfortable with risks that make negotiators feel uncomfortable" Steve Gates, Chief Executive, Gap Partnership

One of the reasons that these factors are important is that people who make big concessions raise the expectations of the other party. People who give a little at a time get the best results. So you need to view concessions through the eyes of the other party in order to manage them. Remember, what the other party thinks is small is as important as what you think is small. Get into their head. Be them!

There are a few related tips that I would share with you about managing concessions. They should be read in conjunction with 5.5.

■ Identify what delivers satisfaction to the other party. It might be about today; it might be about the long term; it might be about the package; it might be about one item. Play the card that turns them on. Anticipate their reaction and modify your approach accordingly.
■ Don't telegraph your concession pattern. Anything that makes you predictable makes it easy to counter your best moves.
■ If any concession – and the package linked to it – is not accepted, don't feel bound to re-present it. You are entitled to withdraw all of it.
■ It is possible to make concessions without actually giving anything away. If you listen attentively to someone's point for twice as long as you want to, you have conceded something to the other party, and that could enhance the negotiation.

## To manage concessions effectively, start small on a small issue.

# 5.5

# Make concessions work for you

We've looked at the need for small concessions, but there are other aspects of concessions that are crucial if you are to secure the outcomes that you want.

The way you manage concessions will affect not only you. It will affect the aspirations of the other party, it will affect their behaviour towards you, and it will surely have a profound effect on the outcome. These tips will help you reach a profitable agreement:

**1** Give yourself room to manoeuvre. Don't leave your initial demands too near to your final objective. In other words, give yourself room to negotiate. Start high if you're selling, and low if you're buying. Have a good reason for starting where you do.

**2** Get all the other party's demands on the table. Get them to open up first. Initially, keep some of your demands hidden. Again, this is to give yourself room to manoeuvre.

**3** Never assume you know what the other party wants. Discover the realities of the situation by the use of good questions. You will make serious mistakes if you proceed on the wrong basis.

**4** Get something for every concession. Never give a concession without securing a concession in return. A concession granted too easily gives the other party less satisfaction than the concession they work hard for.

**5** Let the other person make the first concession, especially on the major issues. You could be first to make minor concessions. Remember later is better than now. The more the other party waits the more they will appreciate the concession.

**6** Don't go in for tit-for-tat concessions, and don't split things 50/50. If you become known as a 50/50 merchant, then people will know exactly where to pitch their demands.

**7** If you can't get a concession, then do your best to get a promise from your negotiating partner.

**8** Don't accept the other party saying, "Sorry, I can't concede that on principle." Such principles usually have no foundation; your job is to test how much the principle is worth.

**9** Keep asking the question, "How much closer to agreement does this concession bring us?" If the answer is not much, don't offer the concession.

**10** If your concessions are not accepted, withdraw them. Don't ever let anybody accept one part of a package which offers a concession, and reject the others. Unless your package is accepted in full, go back to the previous position and try again.

## Recognize that your concessions affect their concessions, and vice-versa.

# 5.6

# Focus on solutions not problems

We touched on how we all see the world through different eyes in 1.4. Some people see problems where others see opportunities. But if we are to reach agreement, it is important to be positive, to look for opportunities that will lead to solutions.

In my experience, buyers tend to be far more negative than sellers. Buyers can defend, just state the problem and sit back and wait for sellers to make the running. So, let's look at how to deal with people who tend to focus on problems. The answer is to be positive, and show the other party how you both being positive will promote agreement.

**1** Have a vision for you and your business. Start with the end in mind. "Let's take stock, Anita. Today we aim to reach an agreement that allows us to work together for the next 12 months. We need to agree a package today because your place in the market, and ours, demands it."

**2** Believe in yourself and what you are trying to do. "We're in good shape to achieve this I think. What do you think, Anita?" Or "I feel we can reach agreement now. How do you see it?"

**3** Surround yourself with positive people when you prepare or when you negotiate. "Who will help you implement this, Anita?"

**4** Turn negatives into positives. Create options. Generate fresh ideas to solve problems (see Secret 6.1). "That seems to be a problem, Anita. If we put buffer stock in place, would that sort it?"

**5** Be realistic and positive but not stupid. "Do you agree with me that this is realistic for both of us?"

**6** Be mindful of pace. Be patient, because being over pushy may make the other party uncomfortable. Being too laid back, though, will cause the negotiation to lose momentum. "What progress are we making, Anita?"

The words we use have a major impact on how the other person responds. Positive words prompt positive thoughts from the other party. The words that persuade someone to your way of thinking are not 'can't' or 'won't'. Someone's name, 'you', 'we', 'us' and 'together' are all powerful words because they bring people together.

Some of the most powerful words in the English language are ones like: easy, simple, new, money, safe, secure, protected, save, retain, health, strength, results, benefits, discover, guarantee, free and promise.

Make sure you have a good stock of positive words, and use them in combination for even more impact. e.g. "This is a new way to save you money."

# Think positively and use positive language to encourage your negotiating partner to think positively too.

# 5.7

# Always secure a counter-proposal

Never modify your proposal without extracting a counter-proposal from the other party. This is something I see happening all the time – and people are totally unaware of it. The consequences can be disastrous. If you don't secure a counter-proposal, you are completely undermining your credibility.

Imagine this situation: you make a proposal; your negotiating partner talks around it but doesn't make a counter proposal; then you get sucked into making another proposal. You've made two proposals and they've made none. What has happened?

■ You have sent a signal that your proposals are not serious.
■ You have sent a signal that suggests that if they want the best deal, all they have to do is shut up, let you do all the running, and you will progressively reduce your demands.
■ You have totally undermined your credibility, because you have demonstrated that you are not negotiating in a structured way.
■ You are making things easy for the other party, which could reduce their satisfaction with the outcome of the negotiation.

# "Quite often, your indifference can be the greatest negotiating weapon you have"

**Max Markson, Australian publicity agent**

There is a related point here, and that is what you should do when the other party comes back with an outrageous demand. In this situation, under no circumstances should you respond. If you offer a counter-proposal to a ridiculous offer, you are giving credibility to that offer. What you need to do is to get them to make a second, more reasonable proposal. Here are some of your options:

- Ignore it completely. (See the quote above.)
- Dismiss it with a laugh.
- Ask them to repeat it (it will usually be watered down when repeated).
- Ask a question.
- Walk out.
- Go back to the previous point that you were discussing.
- Whatever you do, don't offer a proposal. Get them to make a serious proposal.

This seems a good place to focus on the classic good guy/bad guy tactic which may be used against you. You are negotiating with two people. One (the good guy) is reasonable and predictable. The other (the bad guy) makes outrageous demands to disturb your thinking. The counter is the same as outlined above: ignore it, or dismiss it, etc. One counter is to meet them head on and say, "Why are you two playing good guy/bad guy with me?"

## Wait for a serious counter-proposal before you modify your package.

# 5.8

# Use fair procedures

A win-win outcome is dependent on both parties feeling that they have been treated fairly. The other party should feel that fairness has ruled, so this is a vital part of shaking hands on an agreement.

If people feel that they have not been treated fairly, they will feel resentful. They may not reach agreement, or may feel resentful even though they have shaken hands on a deal (a classic win-lose situation).

Along with fair procedures, we should include the use of sources of data that both you and your negotiating partner accept together. Let's look at some examples of using fair procedures and sources of data. If you use these, or your own examples of fair data, you should be able to create win-win agreements.

**case study** International negotiations on the Law of the Sea became deadlocked over the issue of how to allocate deep-sea mining sites. Under the draft agreement, half the sites were to be mined by private companies, the other half by Enterprise, an organization owned by the United Nations. Since the private companies from the rich nations had the technology and expertise to choose the best sites, the poorer

■ **Market value.** There may be a respected publication that you can both agree will define the value of a car, or an exchange rate (say, the *Financial Times*), or the salary for a particular job.

■ **Accepted indices.** If you are negotiating price rises or price reductions, you could refer to government statistics on inflation or the cost of a specific product.

■ **What a court would decide.** You may be able to agree based on what you both think a court ruling would give you. And it might save you going there!

■ **Precedent.** If you can point to something that has been done in a similar situation, it could prompt agreement. An example of this might be a commercial agreement elsewhere in your market.

■ **Equal treatment.** You could point to the fact that other people in a similar position have been offered the same. So it must be reasonable!

■ **Published standards.** You might find that a professional body has published the best way to do things. In the UK, for example, there are construction industry standards that cover many things, including how to make staged payments on a project.

# You and the other party need to come up with fair procedures and accepted sources of data.

nations feared the less knowledgeable Enterprise would receive a bad bargain. The solution was to agree that a private company seeking to mine the seabed would present Enterprise with two proposed mining sites. Enterprise would pick one for itself and grant the company a licence to mine the other. Since the company would not know which site it would get, it had an incentive to make both sites as promising as possible.

# 5.9

# Constantly compare your objectives

You enter a negotiation with objectives. So does the other party. Your discussions will cause your objectives to change. You must learn how to manage the process so that you keep control and don't get lost.

What is going on in most business negotiations is complex, or at least it should be if you are doing it right. Think about what is being discussed – your initial objectives; the other party's version; new issues cropping up; unexpected behaviour; concessions from both parties; complex packages; outrageous demands. Here is another case for bringing out the calculator to help you understand what has happened, what's happening right now, and where you want to go. If you think it's simple, you will be missing something vital. Here's how to manage it.

**1** Constantly re-assess your own objectives and those of your negotiating partner.

**2** Relate this to what movement has taken place on each negotiating variable, for you and for them. This is about tracking who's made what concessions on each issue, and how much this is worth to each of you, plus how much it has cost each of you.

**"**Failure comes only when we forget our ideals and objectives and principles**"** **Jawaharlal Nehru, first Prime Minister of India**

**3** Keep asking yourself "What do I want?" (What am I asking for?) and "What do I need?" (What I must have). Ask, "What are the wants and needs of the other party?"

**4** Keep thinking about the table that you prepared in 2.1 and keep updating it to keep your thinking straight.

**5** In particular, recognize the significance of each new variable introduced. What will it cost? What is it worth to you? What is it worth to them? How significant is it in comparison with all the other variables?

Make a judgement as to whether a likely settlement is acceptable to you. To do this you must know your BATNA (best alternative to a negotiated agreement). You will see reference to it in hundreds of books. It's part of negotiation language, and here's how it fits with this Secret:

■ Is your best alternative to simply walk away?
■ Is your best alternative to do a deal with someone else?
■ Should you do something other than negotiate? How about the alternatives in 1.2, such as postponement, arbitration or pleading?

The point is, you cannot reliably make a decision about your alternatives unless you are aware of what your BATNA is, and use the thought processes and calculations in points 1 to 5 above.

## Use your preparation framework to monitor progress towards agreement.

# 5.10

# Counter the 'nibble'

Just when you think you have agreed a package, you might fall victim to a last-minute 'nibble'. Suddenly the other side produces a variable that you have lost sight of or haven't even considered. Here's how to avoid being caught out.

A 'nibble' is one of those terms that is part of negotiating language all over the world. It means nibbling away at what you thought was an agreement, when in fact you had no basis for agreement at all. You can use it to your advantage, but, at all costs, avoid being hurt by it. It is a good idea to read the case study below first. It gives a good picture of a nibble in action. Let's now consider (a) how you might employ a 'nibble' yourself and (b) how you can counter it.

**case study** A friend of mine called Ron sold second-hand cars and lorries. He had been in his yard for over an hour haggling with a man over a lorry, trading packages that included these variables: price, future servicing, tax, a fresh MOT (test certificate), and method of payment. The man was within £15 of a price of £5,115. Ron said, "OK, it's yours at £5,100," and they

How to use the nibble:

■ First you need to decide whether it is ethical for you to do this.

■ If you decide it is, then you consciously keep a negotiating variable, (or variables!) off the table until the other party thinks you have reached agreement.

■ You are relying on the fact that they will be feeling good because they think they have an agreement. They are vulnerable and you are about to show them that they are!

■ You would be advised to consider whether you want to do business with this person again.

How to counter the nibble:

■ Monitor the progress that has been made on all the variables in your package and that of your partner. Track all the concessions that have been offered and their value to you and to the other side.

■ Check whether there is anything else that should be discussed within the final package (see the case study).

■ Do not agree to a final package until you're sure the other party has put all their cards on the table. If a substantial nibble emerges at the last moment, then you will have to go back to square one.

# Get every issue on the table to counter the nibble.

shook hands. At that the guy said, "Great, fill her up with petrol and I'll be off." The tank of petrol was worth £200! It broke the deal and they parted with bad feeling, both having wasted their time. We could debate the ethics of the case, but if Ron had said at the £5,115 stage, "Before we tie up this sale, is there anything else we need to agree on?", they could have had a deal.

# Find common ground

**You now need to reach** the common ground that is the basis for agreement and to know when to close. This chapter underlines the importance of keeping all the negotiating variables linked in one package. As a successful negotiation nears its close, you should try to spot issues that have arisen that are important to both parties and will bring you together in agreement. You must always make sure that your final agreement is exactly what both parties think it is.

# 6.1

# Invent options for mutual gain

It is good to keep things up your sleeve in order to clinch agreement when the time is right. You can hold back on presenting one of your negotiating variables until it will have maximum impact, or you can come up with new ideas that benefit both parties.

The first of these approaches we have already touched on a couple of times. You hold back until such time as you think that an extra concession will be sufficiently attractive to your negotiating partner to allow them to accept your package. There is an element of your partner being pleasantly surprised by this.

The second way that we can pleasantly surprise the other party is to invent options for mutual gain. This means coming up with new ideas that are beneficial for both parties. One way to look at this is to say that it is not good enough to assume that the size of the cake is fixed – that the purpose of the negotiation is to decide on who gets what share of the cake. No! Try making the cake bigger first.

Two sisters quarrelled over an orange. Finally they decided to split it in half. The first sister took her half, ate the fruit and threw away the peel. The second threw away the fruit and used the peel in her baking. They both 'left money on the table'. It was not a case of win-win!

# "Have more than you show; speak less than you know"

**William Shakespeare, English playwright**

The smart negotiator thinks of new negotiating variables that add value to both parties – that is, they increase the size of the cake. The even smarter negotiator realizes when to put this new card on the table for maximum effect in order to close the deal. What can you do to increase your chances of thinking this creatively?

■ **Prepare.** Preparation will give you a solid base from which to assess the value of each issue.

■ **Have empathy.** Keep asking questions. Keep putting yourself in the other person's shoes, and see if you can come up with issues that are important to both of you.

■ **Be flexible.** By all means prepare, but be open to new ideas as they crop up in the discussion.

■ **Don't get salami-ed.** To get salami-ed is the total opposite of what we are looking at here.

■ **Tie it up in a package.** Your new idea is no good on its own – it will add value to both of you if it is wrapped up in a package that prompts agreement.

■ **Have a win-win mentality.** Avoid prejudices. Be open to new ideas to increase the size of the cake.

# Be constantly on the look out for new opportunities to expand the 'cake' before sharing it out.

# 6.2

# Link all your issues in the final package

We are moving towards the end of this book, just as you will move towards agreement. But we are not there yet, and this Secret is about you having a total picture of what your agreement will look like. Get this right, and the agreement will work for both of you.

This is about taking the package mentality, and taking it even further. It is about dealing with packages, which by now I hope you take for granted – and then seeing the even bigger picture to make sure that you and your negotiating partner are on the same wavelength.

You need to see the complete inter-relationship between the discussion that you have, the understandings you have, the various items within your package, and the final agreement. It is a complete system that needs to add up to a whole that makes sense to both of you, and that both of you feel comfortable with.

Imagine you are trying to get both parties up onto a plateau where they co-operate and participate together. You need to make sure lots of factors are right – conditions in the room, strategies, motives, questions, listening, interruptions, promises, authority levels, knowledge, demonstrations and other things we have discussed. If you achieve it, you've got the whole system right. And the agreement will stick.

Appreciate that when you finish up with a written agreement, that agreement will not necessarily cover everything that will allow you to work together. There could well be unwritten aspects of the arrangement that come from the understanding that you developed during the discussion. This might be the fact that you will enjoy referrals of new business from the other party (something that would be very difficult for you to check on), or it could be that their sales people will promote your products (again, very difficult to monitor).

You need to be aware that no agreement is completely watertight. It has to be based on mutual trust. In UK law, an agreement on paper is not a contract. It is evidence of a contract, which is based on other things as well – for instance what promises and re-assurances have been verbally given. In the culture in which you operate, different but similar considerations will apply in the sense that a great deal will be down to trust. Culture has a significant effect on how agreements are reached, and how they are put into practice – but trust is at the core of any ongoing relationship.

Recognize, therefore, that sometimes a promise is better than nothing. If someone promises to introduce you to new business, that is better than nothing, even if it isn't incorporated in the actual agreement.

## Look at the really big picture of what it is that you are about to agree.

# 6.3

# Try not to say "take it or leave it"

In 4.7 we discussed whether you should ever offer this ultimatum. In some situations it is appropriate, but there is no need to use those emotive words, which could destroy forever any chance of further business.

You could just say, "That's the best I can do," and this may be a good idea if the other party has no option but to take it, your position in the market place won't allow you to go any further, or you cannot afford financially to go any further. You will have less need to issue this ultimatum if you:

---

**case study** I was working for a large group involved in the distribution of pipes, valves and fittings. They had large open-air storage areas where pipes were moved around. The group had a mixed fleet of petrol and electric trucks. One day I heard a sales lady trying to sell the Operations Manager four electric fork-lift trucks. He said, "Your electric trucks are a bit slow for us." The response from the lady was, "They are slow" (don't panic), "but what are the most important factors

---

■ **Recognize who has the authority to agree.** There is no point in struggling to reach agreement with someone when you should be re-convening with different people.

■ **Overcome objections.** This is a selling skill. If someone rejects your idea, adopt the approach shown in the case study below.

■ **Change something.** If you are stuck on a subject, change the subject and return to it later. Use different words. Stand up. Sit down. Adjourn. These are all good ways of breaking deadlock.

■ **Probe aspirations.** People who want more have more deadlocks. Ask the question, "Why are you risking stalemate because of this?"

■ **Ask for a repeat.** Ask for the package to be repeated. Ask for a question to be repeated. Ask for a threat to be repeated. Usually the repeat will be softer than the first version. Try it.

■ **Don't make it personal.** Sort the problems, not the person.

All these tactics are worth trying before you say, "Take it or leave it". People do not like being boxed in. They do not like being intimidated. Give them options, use your influencing skills and your ability to persuade, and people will return to negotiate with you in future.

# Use good negotiating skills to avoid having to say "Take it or leave it".

in your decision making?" (the open question). The Ops manager said "Overall operating costs, which is very much affected by reliability." The sales lady said, "We know our trucks are slow, but that's not really important to you in your congested yards, so we have put the emphasis on reliability, and also, of course, they are green and contribute to a healthier atmosphere in which your people will work." (Put the objection into perspective and offer compensating factors.)

# 6.4

# Hold your nerve and know when to close

You are getting to the end of the negotiation. There is tension. There is doubt. You need to agree. I am going to look at 'closing' in the sense of reaching agreement, clinching the deal.

Negotiation is full of risk. There is a risk that you fall out. There is a risk that you give too much away. How you play things at this stage is down to your judgement. You will close most effectively if you have done all the things we have looked at in previous chapters. They all affect your ability to close. Especially, listen more than you talk, because talking can reveal a lack of confidence that will be exploited. You should be able to hold your nerve, at the same time reassuring the other side. Here are some straightforward tips on 'closing' the negotiation.

**1** **Be assertive.** It's especially important when you close, because you don't want the other party to feel boxed in. So it's assertive behaviour that works – not submissive and not aggressive.

**2** **Timing is everything.** Only you can judge when to push, and when to tread softly. You can only know how to play things if you really understand the other party.

**3** **Be positive.** "If we can't agree it now, when will we?" Don't be put off by big differences, just focus on closing the gap.

**4** **Be sure you can sell the deal.** Make sure that you will be able to sell the deal to those around you, and help the other party sell the deal to the people around them.

**5** **Don't be intimidated.** Providing you are using the Secrets, you should be in a position to continue until you reach a win-win situation. Have courage!

That's your approach to closing. Now here are a few classic closing techniques that you can use:

■ **The point blank close.** "Are we agreed?" This is a closed question, and at this stage closed questions are vital. If it produces an objection, go back to the open question, "Why…"

■ **The assumptive close.** In other words, act as though it's agreed "OK, let's summarize what we've agreed."

■ **The action close.** This would involve you acting as if agreement is a formality – by picking up a blank pad to summarize the deal, or by standing up and sitting alongside the other party with pad in hand.

■ **The alternative close.** "Shall we tie this up before a coffee, or after?"

■ **The special inducement close.** "If we can tie this up now, I am prepared to throw in this one extra thing…"

■ **The conditional close.** "If I can show you how this meets your criteria, do we have a deal?" or "If I do that, do we have a deal?"

# Knowing when to close is a matter of judgement, identifying the moment when you've reached common ground.

# 6.5

# Be aware of body language

We could have looked at body language anywhere in this book. It is a crucial aspect of communicating and is important from the first meeting right through to closing a deal. It is especially useful in gauging reactions to proposals and concessions and in determining that you have reached common ground with your negotiating partner.

Research has shown that 10% of communication depends on the words you use, 30% on how you say them and 60% on your body language. The precise numbers are not important. What matters is that you read other people's body language and decide what it is telling you and that your own body language can help your cause. Here are just a few examples of how to read body language.

■ **Eye contact.** If someone looks at you only 30% of the time, be prepared for the possibility they are lying. If their eye contact is more than 70% it could mean they find you interesting, or they are being hostile.

■ **The eye rub.** This can indicate lying, but women might rub their eye to avoid making a violent gesture, or they might just have an itch!

■ **Arms crossed.** Crossed arms could be a sign of aggression, or rejection of a point that you have just made.

■ **Palm gestures.** Both palms facing upwards could be a sign of openness.

Don't read too much into body language until you have studied it in greater depth (see Further Reading). You might think that someone who refuses to look you in the eye is lying. That would be a dangerous assumption, but if you see a man rubbing his eye or pulling his collar and avoiding your eye and shifting uneasily in their chair, then it's quite likely he's lying. As far as your own body language is concerned, here are a few tips to help you build a good rapport with those around you:

■ **Be conscious of the first impression you create.** People form 90% of their impression of you in the first 90 seconds of meeting you.

■ **Use people's names with a smile.** First, of course, you should check on how they like to be addressed.

■ **Avoid sitting directly opposite someone.** This applies especially at a square or rectangular table. Ideally sit at 60 degrees at a round table.

■ **Lean forward.** This creates the impression that you are particularly interested in what is being said.

■ **Lean back.** Do this if you want to listen or look confident.

■ **Don't invade people's personal space.** A metre apart would be about as close as you should get – unless the two of you are drafting your agreement, in which case get cosy!

■ **Flinch!** Do this every time a proposal is made to you. It could be a small flinch such as a raised eyebrow, or a shake of the head, or a big flinch such as a loud exclamation, but flinch! This is crucial in some cultures, where passiveness is taken as weakness.

# Recognize that body language can be more important than words.

# 6.6

# Fully agree what's been agreed

You can foul up a hard-won agreement if something goes wrong in interpreting that agreement. Here's the Secret to making sure that the agreement sticks.

We've already discussed in 6.2 that no piece of paper or email can ever capture 100% of your agreement. However, it is important to confirm as many aspects of the agreement as possible so that you don't find yourselves disagreeing about exactly what the agreement meant. Here are some tips to help you nail down the agreement and make it work for both parties.

**1** It is advisable to use words to capture some of the things that are difficult to quantify – "This is based on the understanding that…" or "Our expectation is that after this agreement has run its course, we will be in a position to increase our business together."

**one minute wonder** In all your negotiations, quietly and with a minimum of fuss take control of producing the final agreement.

# "Make every bargain clear and plain, that none may afterwards complain" **Greek proverb**

**2** Produce a bullet-pointed summary of what you have agreed before you part. You can hand-write a few bullet points or print from your laptop. This collection of bullet points brings you together at the end, and helps avoid any misunderstanding later.

**3** Confirm the agreement in writing at a later date, in as much detail as possible.

**4** Make sure that in both these above cases you do the writing. This gives you the power to use words that suit you, and it also allows you to show the draft to other people in your business so that they can check there is nothing missing or nothing problematical in the document. If there is, you can sort it out sooner rather than later.

This is in no sense deceiving the other party. If it were, it would destroy the agreement. This is just a legitimate ploy that you can use to keep control. I've done it at the end of every negotiation I've taken part in over the last 20 years. If you confirm every agreement that you are involved in, it will not remove the need for the other party to agree it, but it will give you great confidence and make a major contribution to giving you the results that you want.

## Make sure you pick up a pen and define the agreement in terms that suit you.

# Put it all together

**This short final chapter** is about making sure that all the individual elements we have considered in the course of the book are combined in a joined-up approach to negotiating. If they are, they should enable you to break down any obstacles to agreement. The last two Secrets focus on the qualities that you need to be an effective negotiator. There is also a check list that will allow you to spot the areas in which you need to develop your negotiating skills.

# 7.1

# Deal with a world that is getting smaller

These days we are increasingly likely to come into contact with people from backgrounds very different to our own. This has implications for how we negotiate. We can use modern communications to help us reach agreement, but only if we allow for different cultures. We looked at culture briefly in 1.6. Now we will take a wider view of how to deal with cultural differences in a shrinking world.

Everyone you deal with is an individual, and stereotyping is dangerous – but someone's cultural or commercial background will inevitably affect their behaviour. You need to anticipate this. With modern technology people are able to run businesses from their home, from different countries, and even from a laptop on the beach. This means you are increasingly likely to do business with people from a different culture. They will behave differently to you, and you need to factor this into your strategy. Here are just a few things to watch out for:

**■ Lies.** One person's lies are acceptable distortions of the truth to others.

**■ Weakness.** Being open, or doing someone a good turn, or making a concession will be seen favourably in some quarters – yet considered a weakness in others. Watch and learn!

**■ Bribes.** What is a bribe in one part of the world is OK in another. Many multi-national companies have clear, published guidelines. Be sure that you know when these are in place, and also when you are negotiating with someone who expects you to bend the rules.

**■ Deadlines.** Quick deals will be considered essential by some people, and unacceptable to others. Very few Japanese will respond well to you upping the pace.

**■ Dealing remotely.** Location will sometimes dictate how you need to communicate, but individual preferences should influence how much you can do by telephone and email. You need to enter into their world, know where they are coming from, and why they do what they do.

**■ Timing.** Choose the best time to negotiate. Ask yourself when you should communicate information to someone – before you meet so that they can reflect on it, or towards the end to clinch agreement?

**■ Information overload.** Too much information to someone may be too little for another. With the Internet we have the capacity to send massive amounts of information prior to or after a negotiation. Differences may be simply down to different individuals, but they could be cultural. You need to make sound judgements based on your reading of the other party.

**■ Change the negotiator.** You will never get on well with everyone. Be courageous enough to consider withdrawing yourself and introducing a fresh negotiator if the chemistry between you and the other party is not good. Sometimes a change of negotiator will improve the chances of reaching agreement.

# Understand why people behave differently, and learn from every experience.

# 7.2

# Remember the key points

This Secret is a reminder of the key aspects of negotiating as laid out in the book so far. It can serve as a quick guide that you can refer to before starting out on a negotiation.

There is a lot of advice contained in each chapter. All this advice is important on occasions, because if you fail to master one Secret that could be the one thing that causes your negotiation to fail – the chain is as strong as the weakest link. However, what I want to do here is pull out the major messages. Mark McCormack (see 2.5) suggested that the person who says "everything is important" is telling me that nothing is important. Some things are more important than others, but eventually the competent negotiator will be comfortable with all 50 Secrets contained in the book. For me these are the major messages:

**1** **Know when to negotiate.** Is negotiating the best thing to do in the situation, or would another tactic be better?

**2** **Prepare clear objectives.** Prepare your objectives, the negotiating variables, and your tactics. The basis of this is defining Desirable/Probable/Worst outcomes.

# "A chain is as strong as its weakest link" Traditional proverb

**3** **Discuss your respective positions.** Put yourself in the other party's shoes. Be them. Get them up on a plateau with you, freely exchanging ideas. Listen more than you talk. Keep asking yourself, "How far apart are we?" and "Where do I want to finish up?"

**4** **Deal only in packages.** Don't get 'salami-ed' by agreeing to different elements one by one.

**5** **Bargain your way to success.** Use "if". If you concede, attach a condition. Ask yourself, "How can I bridge the gap?" But keep a variable or two up your sleeve.

**6** **Find common ground to reach agreement.** Invent options for mutual gain. Link all the issues together in packages.

**7** **Now put it all together.** Review your performance, and consider how you can develop attitudes, skills and knowledge that will make you an even better negotiator.

Those were based on our chapter headings. Two more ideas for you to concentrate on would be to seek win-win solutions if you want a long term relationship, and to be clear about team roles, in both your team and in the other team.

## See the business of negotiating as a complete system where all the component parts need to work together.

# 7.3

# Check your negotiating qualities

If you use this comprehensive list of the qualities needed in an effective negotiator in conjunction with the final Secret, you will learn from every negotiation, your negotiating skills will improve, and so too will the results that you enjoy.

We spoke in 4.8 about the idea that the qualities needed in any situation can be broken down into Attitude, Skills and Knowledge. Bear in mind that your attitude will drive your behaviour, and that, if you want to, you will be able to change your behaviour more quickly than you can change your attitudes (which are more deep seated). Here are the qualities (the tool kit) that you should be looking for in yourself if you want to succeed as a negotiator.

**Attitudes** (Behave like this)
- Be co-operative. Seek win-win outcomes.
- Have empathy. Explore other peoples' interests.
- Be open minded to new ideas.
- Be flexible in your approach.
- Be prepared to accept pressure and face conflict.
- Be assertive, not aggressive not submissive.

- Be prepared to live with doubt, and create certainty from it.
- Be patient.
- Be positive, focused on agreement.
- Be confident, but respect the other party's rights.
- Be motivated to succeed.
- Be a calculated, measured risk-taker.
- Be prepared to learn from every negotiation.

**Skills** (Display these)
- Plan the negotiation, and organize yourself and your time to suit.
- Be numerate and analytical.
- Listen more than you talk.
- See the big picture and pick strategies to suit.
- Ask an appropriate balance of open and closed questions.
- Persuade others with your communications.
- Trade packages based on sound judgments. Track concessions against Desirable/Probable/Worst objectives.
- Gather information on the other party and their situation.
- Solve problems creatively.

**Knowledge** (Make sure you know)
- The other party and their organization.
- The other party's goals and aspirations.
- The market in which you both operate.
- Your competition.
- Your products.
- The limits of responsibility of yourself and the other party.
- When to summarize.
- When to adjourn.

# This tool kit of attitudes, skills and knowledge will help you achieve success as a negotiator.

# 7.4

# Develop yourself as a negotiator

The previous Secret identified the qualities needed to negotiate successfully. This check list will give you an idea as to where your strengths and weaknesses lie. It will allow you to come up with a plan to improve your skill set for your next negotiation.

You should use this review mechanism to assess your own performance, and even have someone else assess your performance if you negotiated as part of a team. You should be aware of your strengths, and play to them. You should also be aware of those areas that you need to develop, and continuously improve your skills. Rate your performance on each of the bullet-points on the following scale: 0 = awful (get someone else to negotiate for you), 2 = dangerously weak, 4 = in need of attention, 6 = needs further improvement, 8 = good, 10 = superb.

Here are the questions that will allow you to rate yourself:

**1** **Your preparation**
  ■ Did you identify negotiating variables?
  ■ Were your objectives prioritized?
  ■ Were your objectives realistic?

## 2 Achieving your objectives
- Did you settle inside or outside Desirable/Probable/Worst?
- Why did you settle where you settled?
- Was the outcome win-win?

## 3 Your control of the process
- Should you have negotiated at all or should you have used some other process?
- Did you prepare, discuss, bargain, deal in packages, and agree?
- Did you summarize and adjourn when necessary?
- If you negotiated as a team, did you stick to your team roles?

## 4 Understanding the other party
- Did you understand the individual's culture?
- Did you understand the company culture?
- Did you explore their interests and put yourself in their shoes?
- How often did you invent options for mutual gain?

## 5 Your management of packages
- Were all your proposals presented as packages?
- Were all packages fully explored?
- Did you track concessions, trade concessions, and value concessions?

## 6 Your ability with regard to these key qualities
- Focus on agreement.
- Assertiveness.
- Listening to the other party.
- Being flexible.
- Asking an appropriate balance of open and closed questions.
- Being creative.

# Move on to the next negotiation even better equipped than you were before.

# Jargon buster

## ASK
Acronym for Attitude, Skills and Knowledge.

## Bargain
To offer concessions and trade packages until both parties feel they have a package that is acceptable to both of them.

## BATNA
Best Alternative to a Negotiated Agreement. Exactly that – it's the best things you can do if you can't reach an agreement.

## Buffer stock
A quantity of goods or of a commodity kept in store to safeguard against shortages or unforeseen demand.

## Closed question
A question that can only be answered "Yes" or "No".

## Concession
A move by a negotiator that takes them closer to their negotiating partner's position.

## Empathy
The ability to put yourself in someone else's shoes and see things through their eyes.

## Framework
A detailed plan of your objectives and negotiating variables that you should prepare before starting negotiations.

## Movement
Changes in position made by negotiating partners as they make concessions to move closer to agreement.

## Negotiating partner
This is the person that you negotiate with. Sometimes referred to as the other party. I use the word partner because in most business situations we are negotiating with someone that we want to do repeat business with; someone that we want an ongoing relationship with. Partner could be one individual, or a team that you are negotiating with. (Old-fashioned books might refer to opponents – which has little to do with an ongoing relationship.)

## Negotiating variable
Any aspect of the negotiation – e.g. price, quantity, payment terms – on which you can give or take. Any issue on which you can negotiate.

## Nibble
This is yet another demand made by one of the negotiating partners just when you thought you had reached agreement.

## NLP

Neuro-linguistic programming is a collection of techniques that help people communicate more effectively and overcome performance-limiting behaviours.

## Open question

A question beginning "What", "Where", When?', "How" etc. that elicits information from your negotiating partner.

## Outcomes

What you want to finish up with; the results. Could also be called objectives, but outcomes are something that you should be able to visualize.

## Package

This is a collection of negotiating variables. You bargain with packages.

## Strategy

This is how you plan to achieve your objectives. Usually it is about the big things you plan to do, but it could also include the things that you plan not to do.

## Tactics

These are the lower-level actions that come from your objectives and high-level strategy.

## Salami-ed

A situation in which you are prevented from dealing with packages because you have allowed yourself to agree on a series of individual issues.

## Win-win

A situation in which both parties have reason to feel satisfied with the outcome of the negotiation.

# Further reading

There is so much material available on the Internet and in archives, and your needs are special to you. You won't want to read all this material, but you can look at the big ideas. So, search for published material to suit you. Here are pointers to help you.

Anderson, David J. *Agile Management for Software Engineering: Applying the Theory of Constraints for Business Results* (Prentice Hall PTR, 2003) ISBN 013-1424602

Borg, James *Persuasion: the Art of Influencing People* (Pearson Education, 2004) ISBN 978-0-2736-8838-9

Cohen, Steven *Negotiating Skills for Managers* (McGraw Hill Professional, 2002) ISBN 978-0-0713-8757-6

Covey, Stephen R. *7 Habits of Highly Effective People: Powerful Lessons in Personal Change* (Simon and Schuster, 2004) ISBN 978-0743272452

Denny, Richard *Succeed for Yourself: Unlock Your Potential for Success and Happiness* (Kogan Page 3rd Edition, 2009) ISBN 978-0-7494-5644-3

Goleman, Daniel *Working with Emotional Intelligence* (Bloomsbury Publishing, 1999 ) ISBN  978-0-7475-4384-8

Hindle, Tim *Negotiating Skills*  (Dorling Kindersley, 1998) ISBN 978-0-7513-0531-9

Karrass, Chester L. *Give and Take* (Ty Crowell Co, 1974) ISBN 978-0-6900-0566-0

Karrass, Chester L. *The Negotiating Game* (HarperCollins) ISBN 978-0-8873-0709-6

Kotter, John P. and Chen, Dan S. *The Heart of Change: Real-Life Stories of How People Change Their Organizations* (Harvard Business School Press, 2002) ISBN 978-1-5785-1254-6

Markides, Constantinos C. *All the Right Moves: A Guide to Crafting Breakthrough Strategy* (Harvard Business School Press, 1999) ISBN 978-0-8758-4833-4

McCormack, Mark H. *What They Don't Teach You At Harvard Business School!* (Profile Business, 1994) ISBN 978-1861975645

McCormack, Mark H. *What They Still Don't Teach You At Harvard Business School!* (Bantam, 2001) ISBN 978-0-5533-4961-0

McCormack Mark H. *What You'll Never Learn on the Internet* (Harper Collins Business, 2000) ISBN 978-0-0025-7171-5

Pease, Allan and Barbara *The Definitive Book of Body Language: How to Read Others' Attitudes by Their Gestures* (Orion, 2005) ISBN 978-0-7528-5878-4

Shapiro, Mo *Understanding Neuro-linguistic Programming in a Week* (Hodder & Stoughton, 1998) ISBN 978-0-3407-1123-1

Wileman, Andrew *Driving Down Cost: How to Manage and Cut Costs - Intelligently* (Nicholas Brealey Publishing, 2008) ISBN 978-1-8578-8512-5

The author's approach to negotiating and performance management is viewable at www.scott-brown.co.uk. Details of David Brown's workshop *Improve Your Negotiating Skills* can be obtained by emailing David at davidbrown@scott-brown.co.uk.

www.BusinessSecrets.net